White Collar Unemployment

Wiley Series on
Organizational Change and Development

Series Editor

Professor Iain Mangham

*Centre for the Study of Organizational
 Change and Development
University of Bath
Claverton Down
Bath*

White Collar Unemployment
Impact and Stress

Stephen Fineman

Further titles in preparation

White Collar Unemployment

Impact and Stress

Stephen Fineman
University of Bath
Centre for Study of Organizational Change
and Development

JOHN WILEY & SONS
Chichester · New York · Brisbane · Toronto · Singapore

Library of Congress Cataloging in Publication Data

Fineman, Stephen.
  White collar unemployment.

  (Wiley series on organizational change and
development)
  Includes bibliographical references and index.
  1. White collar workers.   2. Unemployed.
I. Title.   II. series.
HD5718.M39F56   1983   331.13′7804   82-8590

ISBN 0 471 10490 6

British Library Cataloguing in Publication Data

Fineman, Stephen
  White collar unemployment.—(Wiley series on
  organizational change and development)
  1. Unemployed   2. White collar workers
  I. Title
  306′.36   HD5708

  ISBN 0 471 10490 6

Typeset by Inforum Ltd, Portsmouth
Printed in Great Britain by the Pitman Press Ltd., Bath, Avon

To

Rona, Daniel, and Anna

Acknowledgements

I am indebted to several people who have helped to make this book possible. The fieldwork would not have happened without George Heaviside's generous welcome and assistance. Iain Mangham and Chris McGivern provided thoughtful criticism of my manuscript — their comments helped to shape its final form. Jean Honebon patiently read, reflected upon, and typed what I had written. My thanks to you all.

Contents

Series Preface

Over the past twenty years or so, there has been an explosion of interest in the social and psychological aspects of human activity in organizations. Courses on organizational behaviour are now commonplace in institutions of higher education. New departments have been created and a series of disciplines or schools have come into existence to dispute the grand claim to be guardians of the eternal verities, and prosecute the research.

This series of books seeks to report, in as non-partisan a fashion as possible, the results of the research, to extend the ideas, concepts and approaches to the study of organizations, and the processes of change and development which occur within and around them. The emphasis throughout will be upon the study and understanding of human experience and conduct within institutions of all kinds; contributions which bear upon this from scholars in organizational sociology, organizational behaviour, organizational development, organizational psychology, social administration, industrial relations, anthropology, linguistics or whatever will be welcome.

The present volume, the first in the series, offers some interesting insight into conduct within organizations as revealed by a study of those currently without employment. The world-taken-for-granted that is so much part of the warp and weft of the employed person's conduct is here revealed to be one of the more important threads which hold views of self and worth in place. The study challenges some of the more facile notions of motivation and work experience and offers some insights into the meaning of work from the perspective of those deprived of it.

Chapter 1

Introduction

This book is about the impact of unemployment on people hitherto relatively immune to such a happening—white collar workers. It concerns what people such as professionals and managers feel like without jobs, what type of adjustments they have to make, and the legacy it leaves with them. It presents images of some of the pains and pleasures of being jobless from the perspective of the 'victim' and also his near relatives and friends. It also reflects on things we might be able to do in the circumstances.

My curiosity about the plight of the unemployed white collar worker was kindled some 5 years ago as an occupational guidance counsellor with recently unemployed managers and professionals. This was a period of escalating unemployment in the United Kingdom, a growth which shows no sign of diminishing today. Current estimates suggest that white collar workers still represent a relatively small fraction of the total unemployed—about 9 per cent. Yet such a figure can all too easily be used to overlook what is happening to a lot of people, approximately 200,000 at the present time (*Employment Gazette*, August 1981).

During my counselling I was particularly struck by the *range* of reactions to the unemployment predicament, from utter depression to positive exuberance. Of around 40 clients I noticed a fairly even spread across these extremes. From the little I then recalled about the research on the psychological effects of unemployment, typical reactions were more characteristically of shock, distress, and anxiety—a uniformly bleak picture, exacerbated by prolonged unemployment. A deeper delving into the literature confirmed my general impression, but it also revealed that the vast majority of research was on blue collar workers during the Depression of the 1930s. I could find few systematic studies on the psychological effects of unemployment for white collar groups. There were a number of articles in business magazines and several newspaper reports by investigative journalists. But putting these fragments of information together, the picture was still one of the negative, stressful nature of job loss.

This left me with lots of unanswered questions. What accounted for the range of feelings I detected during my counselling? Were the managers and professionals all, in fact, much-injured people, but some were unwilling to admit such to themselves or to me? Or was it more to do with the *different* meanings that unemployment can have for different people—influenced by their prior work experience and life position? Would they not be more involved in their work than blue collar workers? What about the influence of specific personality variables, such as personal stability, fear of failure, and the need to achieve? Managers and professionals, as a middle class group, should be more financially protected than others, but on the other hand they are likely to have greater financial commitments. Would not all these factors contribute to their reactions to unemployment?

And so on. Much remained to be resolved. In particular I required some framework to help me link together at least some of these features. This would assist me in my understanding of what was going on, and why reactions to unemployment could vary so. While there were no shortage of psychological and sociological frameworks which could be of assistance, I instinctively turned to a research area in which I had already worked and had some personal investment —stress.

Many of the responses I had observed amongst my clients could be readily characterized in terms of stress—or more accurately by the presence or absence of stress. Those who reported stress either used that very term, or had a recognizable symptomatology. For example, chronic anxieties, depression, feelings of worthlessness, and hopelessness. This was, for some, accompanied by more physical manifestations such as high blood pressure, heart disease, skin complaints, and digestive problems. I tried to differentiate variations in stress response to unemployment using a generic, psychosocial model of stress. The relevant details of this model appear later in the book, but its essence is to view stress in terms of the consequences of an individual's failure to effectively master threatening problems. This did help me—some things fell into place. For example, many of the managers and professionals who had reported a high level of stress felt particularly threatened by their unemployment because of their deep involvement in their previous job, and the belief that they were managing so well. Moreover, some were overcommitted financially, a burden which felt all the greater when a spouse was generally unsympathetic. But as worrying as this might be, the chronic condition of stress emerged from failing to remove the threat. Either there was an inability to enter the job market, or there had been successive failures when doing so. In contrast, those experiencing little or no stress were not threatened by their job loss. They certainly had a problem to solve—finding a new job; but for many this was viewed as a welcome opportunity to reform their lives. Unlike the stressed individuals, few were particularly committed or involved in the job they had lost, and many elected for redundancy.

While all this seemed to make some sense, I still felt I had only scratched the surface of my field of enquiry. There were three reasons for this. Firstly, my conclusions were based upon a fairly small number of people. I required far more intensive qualitative and quantitative data on the spectrum of subjective meaning, threat, and impact associated with unemployment. Secondly, I wished to systematically follow up the managers and professionals to chart any changes in their fortunes, experience, and adaptation. Finally, I was keen to get some indication of how others see their problems, particularly those nearest, and dearest, who have unwittingly become part of the event.

This book describes the outcome of this venture. It is based upon the experiences of 100 managers and professionals who agreed to be participants in counselling and research (intervention research), and also my own experiences in working with them. The 100 gives much scope for individualistic analysis and qualitative interpretation. It also lends itself to statistical analysis where quantitative data have been gathered. Yet I make no claims for the 'representativeness' of the group; it is not that type of study. I am primarily concerned with individuals; their reactions, adaptations, and the differences between them.

Of the chapters to follow, the account of this study is the central focus. Nevertheless, I have sought to place the investigation into its specific context by looking initially at precisely what we do and do not know about the psychological effects of unemployment amongst white collar workers. As the results of the study unfold, and at the end of the book, I speculate on the implications of the findings for action that we might take on unemployment and its consequences. This draws upon one of the accidental discoveries that I made—that the unemployed 'know' about *employment* in a way that many of those who have jobs probably cannot appreciate or express.

The bulk of the findings are derived from the analyses of qualitative data— what participants actually said. To this I have added summary descriptions of the relevant numerical analyses, but for consistency of style and presentation I have placed the associated tables and statistics in the Appendices. The exception to this is Chapter 12 (towards the end of the book) which is based exclusively on a statistical analysis of the data from the quantitative measures. The reader who is not predisposed to 'numbers' and statistics can find a summary of the main points at the end of that chapter and also (more generally) in the final chapter of the book.

It is hoped that this book will be helpful to those trying to understand the meaning, impact, and implications of unemployment amongst white collar workers, including people who have to confront such job loss themselves. It may also be more than a passing curiosity to those whose actions in one way or another shape and regulate employment and unemployment.

Chapter 2

White Collar Unemployment—What We Know

A literature search into the experience of unemployment soon revealed that the mainstream of research emanated from labour economists. Thus 'experience' of unemployment has been conceptualized and measured in terms of variables such as sex, type of skill, period of unemployment, earnings before and after unemployment, sources of information used about new jobs, and job search strategies undertaken. These categories present a somewhat 'clean', actuarial image of the unemployed, usually circumscribed by a rational model of job market behaviour; they miss (and do not usually intend to hit) the feelings and patterns behind the categories—the quintessence of unemployment.

Other social scientists who one might expect to have filled this gap (particularly psychologists and sociologists) do not seem to have found unemployment a very inspiring research topic, judging from the dearth of publications. In the 1930s their output reached a zenith—there are 112 publications listed in a 1938 review article by Eisenberg and Lazarsfeld. There has been some re-emergence of interest in recent years, but with little systematic thrust or effort.

Looking specifically at white collar unemployment, the available literature is even thinner. This may be because white collar unemployed are generally in the statistical minority of any pool of unemployed; they therefore become a less attractive 'social problem' for research and research funding. But this, of course, is little solace for many *individuals*, whose problems are very real to them.

I propose to try to synthesize the available literature on the impact of unemployment on white collar workers in this chapter; mainly because it sets into context the study which follows, but also because it is interesting to assess how far we have got already. I view the literature on blue collar unemployment as less central to the theme of this book. However some of the patterns and

4

principles which exist are relevant to our discussions, so these will be dealt with in summary form towards the end of the chapter.

But firstly to briefly clarify a few terms. In practice 'white collar' is a convenient label to describe people whose occupations are characteristically professional, administrative, or managerial. People who are likely to be responsible for the supervision or welfare of others and have specific skills and knowledge, often acquired from a lengthy period of education and training. So we are talking about teachers, engineers, managing directors, sales executives, personnel managers, sales managers, bankers, and retail supervisors—to mention but a few. By 'unemployed' I refer to the situation where these people are without paid work usually following the loss of a job. Some, though, are unemployed having never experienced work in their field of interest.

The impact on white collar unemployed

I was able to locate a total of 30 research papers concerned in part, or whole, with a specific empirical investigation into the effects of, or reaction to, unemployment amongst white collar workers. Of these, 15 were 'serious' research investigations, the remainder comprised speculative articles based upon casual empiricism, or were restatements—an author's re-presentation of findings he or she had published elsewhere.

Three clear orientations were discernible amongst these studies. The first was that job loss was inevitably, and dominantly, a trauma for white collar workers, resulting in a severe negative reaction. The second was that the trauma response progressed through a series of relatively fixed phases, each with different characteristics. And the final one emphasized the non-uniformity and contingent nature of reactions.

The universal trauma

This is the most popular image of the effects of job loss (15 of the 30 reports). It is also the one most frequently featured in the non-technical literature.

The typical assumption underpinning the trauma hypothesis is that white collar workers are so firmly wedded to their jobs that separation invariably causes a severe emotional shock (the 'trauma') which produces a lasting psychological disturbance. Their self-image is intimately tied in with their job in ways uncharacteristic of other occupational groups. So to lose one's job means to lose part of one's identity, resulting in confusion and disorientation— uniformly *negative* reactions. Groups higher up the occupational ladder, it is contended, are particularly prone to such reactions because of the strong personal investment in progressive career-building, coupled with expectations of job security and tenure. The white collar worker, in giving himself to his job in this way, risks losing his status, prestige, and a main focus of his life if he loses his job—things which are not easily replaced. Such is the intensity of the loss that some liken it to facing the death of a loved one.

The lone early study in this arena was conducted by Hall in 1933. Comparing a group of 360 unemployed professional engineers with a matched group of employed professionals he noted that the level of morale amongst 75 per cent of the unemployed was generally poorer, and antagonism towards employers as a class greater amongst 68 per cent of them, than the comparison group. (An interesting additional result was that those in his employed sample who anticipated job loss had a morale as depressed as those already out of work). Hall's findings have some parallels with Wedderburn's survey of 139 redundant white collar workers, conducted 31 years later. She concludes from her structured interview data that around 60 per cent reacted with shock and anxiety, and adds: 'No statistical account can hope to reflect the anxiety and worry which an event like the loss of job causes' (p. 19). Wedderburn also notes how unfairly rewarded some felt for the loyalty and hard work they had given, and how the older men felt particularly hard hit because of their belief that their age would be a handicap in the job market.

Estes (1973) studied 200 unemployed professionals, comparing them with a control group of 100 continuously employed professionals. He found the unemployed preoccupied with self-blame and personal recrimination which persisted throughout their unemployment and after a new job had been secured. He concludes that job loss creates a situation 'replete with intra-psychic and interpersonal turmoil' (p. 176). There was a loss of central life interest resulting in social withdrawal, a reduction in the strength of community ties, and higher rates of family break-up than was found with employed professionals. Such an image is consistent with the less formal observations of Maurer (1979), Kets de Vries (1978), Oates (1972), Mines (1979), and Porter (1977), who speak of the bitterness, loneliness, helplessness, despondency, loss of self-respect, and 'ego shattering' effect of job loss, particularly if it is a sudden event.

Braginsky and Braginsky (1975) detail the nature of the trauma more specifically, and support Estes' (1973) finding concerning the legacy of its effects after re-employment. They interviewed 46 jobless men and 54 employed men of similar background and age, many of whom held managerial or engineering positions. The majority of the unemployed had had 20 years of prior steady work before losing the jobs. When interviewed they had been unemployed an average of 6 months. The researchers found that most felt unwanted by society; felt small, insignificant, and unknown, dehumanized and degraded by the bureaucracy of unemployment agencies; confused, disillusioned, and betrayed. They experienced family tensions and would shun social company because of their shame. Those who were able to return to work felt more valuable to society, but their cynicism about society had significantly increased. Findings from some other studies repeat this general theme, but with slight variations. The increasing debilitation and anxiety amongst higher-status level unemployed is reported by Goodchilds and Smith (1963) and Shanth-amani (1973). Estes and Wilensky (1978) note, however, that financial pressures may be an important ingredient in such reactions.

A labour market survey of 867 UK unemployed professionals and exec-utives (Berthoud, 1979) has a short section on the personal feelings of the unemployed. The majority reactions reported range from unpleasant to severe distress, shame, and degradation, aggravated as time out of work increases. While acute hardship was absent, most felt the pressures of money shortage, and the attendant social embarrassment.

Together these studies appear to suggest that the loss of job is especially traumatic to white collar workers. But this seductively uniform picture is blurred somewhat by studies reporting more equivocally.

As part of a broader investigation into unemployment Schlozman and Verba (1979) looked at the level of trauma and consequent stress experienced by their respondents. They conducted a telephone survey of 1370 people, 571 of whom were jobless. They then followed up 60 of the unemployed in personal interviews. Like previous investigators they found reports of psychological stress to be common—nervous tension, difficulty sleeping, frequent headaches, fears about the future, and loss of self-confidence and self-esteem. Those unemployed reporting trauma considerably outnumbered those not experien-cing such effects. But, contrary to the investigators' expectations, the *more* prestigious the job lost, the *less* psychologically devastating was the response. The researchers attempt to explain this finding by suggesting that the pro-fessional retains his sense of professional identity after unemployment in a way in which the unemployed non-professional does not. The 'profession' lives on.

The work of Little (1973, 1976) casts further doubts on universality, and extremity, of the professional's trauma. Starting with the assumption that middle class unemployment ought to be especially threatening for American males because of the high value placed upon occupational achievement, he interviewed 100 unemployed technical professionals and compared them with the questionnaire responses of 40 employed professionals. Perhaps his most striking finding is that 48 per cent of the 100 unemployed had a *positive* attitude towards job loss, an attitude reflecting factors such as general optimism about the future, relief from the stressful demands of work, and a needed stimulus or challenge. Little appears to be in rather a dilemma as to what to make of this. On the one hand he feels that unemployment *should* be threatening for professionals, therefore the positive reactions must be a manifestation of psychological defence—coping with the inconsistency between a 'competent professional' image and 'unemployed' (Little, 1973). However, in a later (1976) paper, he chooses to emphasize his results as evidence for 'middle class adaptability'. Freeing oneself awhile from the trappings of the *a priori* trauma hypothesis, it is tempting to conclude that 46 out of 100 people are perhaps not simply engaging in psychological defence.

Hartley (1980) tackles the hypothesis in rather a different way, by focusing on the effects of unemployment on self-esteem. She compared the self-esteem of 87 unemployed middle and senior managers with 64 employed managers using a self report questionnaire and interviews. In both cross-sectional and longitudinal analyses no statistical differences could be found: self-esteem was not lower amongst the unemployed managers and did not decline with longer unemployment.

Trauma—a summary overview

There seems to be a fairly well-founded case that unemployed white collar workers *can* report reactions consistent with the event being traumatic for them. The moot point is the extent of universality of this phenomenon. Some starkly contradictory studies lend some reasonable doubt to its generality. Furthermore, if we are curious about numerical minorities in the existing investigations, then even the apparently most supportive studies look less clear-cut. For example, 25 per cent of Hall's 1933 unemployed sample did not have 'poorer morale' and 40 per cent of Wedderburn's group did not report anxiety reactions. Other studies are conspicuous by their failure to report minority reactions. One certainly gains the impression that some investigators are perhaps over-keen to 'prove' that unemployed white collar workers *are* in shock, whatever.

One explanation that feelings of devastation may not be a universal response is that reactions to unemployment may be sequentially phasic. So there may be several *different* facets of reaction passed through over time. Let us examine studies of this genre.

Phasic reactions

Several writers have based their phasic analysis of reactions to unemployment on the life crisis model proposed by Fink (1967). Fink suggests that in any life crisis (defined as a period when one is unable to cope with stress using one's normal repertoire of responses) one moves through four sequential stages of response—shock, defensive retreat, acknowledgement, and adaptation. This model has been adopted by Harrison (1973) for analysing the reactions of redundant managers whom he views as being in a crisis situation characterized by 'massive disruptions which are almost invariably traumatic and far reaching in their psychological effects' (p. 78). Working from the statements of others who have counselled redundant managers he concludes that each of Fink's stages is passed through by everyone, at a pace proportional to the severity of the initial trauma. This type of analysis is supported by Beer and Swaffin-Smith (1976) who would 'rejuvenate the redundant manager' by tailoring their intervention to the particular Fink stage in which the manager finds himself.

Hayes and Nutman (1981) place a heavy emphasis on the notion of job loss being a period of 'psycho-social transition' characterized by phases of reaction.

One of their preferred frameworks is culled from the work of Hopson and Adams (1976) who studied 100 people who had undergone various life transitions. Seven phases were identified. The first was one of *immobilization*, being overwhelmed by the event. Then a *minimization* stage characterized by a denial of the reality of the event. As a new reality increasingly emerges a state of *depression* develops. Gradually, though, there can be an *acceptance of a changed reality*, where people start to *test out* their new life. This can lead to a *search for meaning* which, if successful, is *internalized* to become part of a new self-image. Hayes and Nutman cite their own case experiences and other studies to show that unemployed individuals (white collar and blue collar) can be categorized in this way. But they are also fairly cautious in their evaluation of the validity of the framework.

Some investigators have *derived* stages of responses from their observations of unemployed managers and professionals rather than using an *a priori* scheme. Powell and Driscoll (1973) found four major stages, rather different in quality from Fink's. The first was one of relaxation and relief, glad that their uncertainty was over and optimistic about the future. The second was a period of concentrated effort—well-organized job search. In the penultimate stage, vacillation, doubt and anger began to appear. Job searching would continue, but half-heartedly. Finally, a stage of apathy, listlessness, and cynicism set in; they felt beaten and helpless. The sensitivity of Powell and Driscoll's analysis is compelling. They claim that their stages are typical of human reactions to unemployment—despite small numbers of people in some of the stages in their own study.

The phasic analysis of Finley and Lee (1981) is based upon the view that an unemployed executive experiences conflict and tension between his current and ideal self-image, a feeling as acute in intensity as that experienced during the stages of dying. From their counselling experience and existing literature they propose three sequential stages. The first is a primary stage of shock, leading to denial or disbelief—or even relief if the stress leading up to the unemployment has been considerable. The second response stage is characterized by bargaining, motivated by feelings of disbelief, guilt, and anger. In this stage the executive will try hard to get reinstated in his company, prolonging non-acceptance of his loss. There will be feelings of depression resulting from the inability to make decisions, accompanied by loss of sleep, anxiety, and withdrawal. The final stage is one of acceptance and peace. The mourning is completed and the future is clearer. The writers cite evidence (Gallagher, 1980) that this final stage will usually be reached within 2 weeks of the termination date.

A final study of this ilk is one by Ragland-Sullivan and Barglow (1981), involving an unusual sample for this type of literature—university academics. Like Finley and Lee, they consider the reactions of their sample in terms of a mourning process following a psychological trauma and loss. They base their analysis on letters from American academics who have been denied tenure, and interview material from 13 academics in the same predicament (gathered over a 6-year period). They describe four phases of mourning using a Freudian analytic framework. In the preparatory stage for job loss the academic would begin to feel estranged and cynical about the 'system'; some would frantically engage in their research. During job loss reactions ranged considerably, from temporary paranoia to quiet acceptance; yet all displayed a degree of shock and panic. During their 'one year's notice', the next phase, some would leave academia abruptly, humiliated and ready to escape. Others, whose identity was strongly linked with academia, would strive even more intensely as if to vindicate their competence. Job hunting was found to be a humiliating experience, and some suffered severe clinical depression. The tension and gloom characterizing the drama of the whole event up to this point is forcefully portrayed as follows:

> The emotional atmosphere described repeatedly seemed reminiscent
> of the administering of a death sentence to a condemned murderer,
> with the offering of a terminal teaching year as an analogue to that
> special last meal granted to the criminal. (p. 62)

Adjustment varied in the final phase—the first year away from the university. Most were established in new careers, some considering the benefit of self-insight they had gained from their experience. Others used humour to cope with their loss and anger. Those who had taken non-academic jobs still retained attachment to academic identity, such was the force of its socialization.

Phases—an overview

The studies concerned with phasic reactions to unemployment have one common denominator—the assumption that a primary trauma, crisis, or threatening life situation sets off certain reactions. At this level, therefore, they do not differ from the standard 'trauma' hypothesis and as such may be viewed with the same reservations. However, accepting that the studies have detected trauma (each in their own way) then they certainly enhance our understanding of reactions to unemployment by showing that responses can vary quite considerably over time: the trauma reaction is not necessarily unidimensional. But the form of variation is differently described, as is the likely number of phases and the range and quality of reactions within them.

It seems most plausible that white collar workers will indeed *change* in their response to unemployment over time; they are adapting, reconstruing and learning. If the event is a traumatic one then some form of discernible phases may be passed through. But what these phases look like in quality, quantity, and in time may vary considerably—according (for example) to the circumstances and meaning of the unemployment to those affected, the coping mechanisms adopted, and the success or failure to obtain a new job (or whatever is sought to replace the lost job). It is so far unclear whether the unemployed *experience* moving in and out of phases, or whether the phases represent mere labels of convenience for the observer/investigator. Furthermore it is possible that phases may loop, or be cyclical, rather than linear. Thus the shock of losing a job may be followed by a similarly intense shock later on when one is rejected for a job that 'looked ideal'.

We are now moving towards a position where *differences* may be as (or more) important for understanding the impact of unemployment than a search for similarities and invariant patterns. So reactions need to be viewed within the contingencies and circumstances of the unemployment. A few studies have been conducted in this vein.

Differences and contingencies

The appropriateness of the Fink model of crisis response to unemployed managers is strongly criticized by Huczynski (1978). He contends that managers cannot be treated as a homogeneous group with similar problems and concerns, all suffering identity crises, concerned about status loss and desiring a job as soon as possible. He finds that trauma and threat is characteristic of only the minority of course members with whom he has worked. These he described as *distressants*—anxious, mid-career managers who have had redundancy forced upon them. The majority comprise three main groups: those who have voluntarily left a job in which they were unhappy and are excited about the future; those who have clearly mapped where they are going and why—usually young careerists; and those older managers who have resigned for health reasons or personal differences with superiors and are seeking pastures new. Although a rather impressionistic account, this analysis does draw our attention to the very different personal positions which can lead to contrasting attitudes towards being unemployed.

Swinburne (1981), from a detailed qualitative study of 20 unemployed managers and professionals, speculates a much slower phasic reaction than has been suggested by previous studies. None of her group had reached a stage of pessimism or acceptance despite a few having been unemployed 12 months or over. (The majority, however, had been without a job for 2–6 months). Over half of the sample reported strong feelings of *positive* gain. Feelings of loss were most apparent amongst those whose occupational identity and self-identity were closely entwined.

Swinburne's study is particularly important because it is one of the very few which begins to tease out some of the subtleties of reactions to unemployment. Like Huczynski, she notes how managers and professionals are not always slaves to their calling, so the trauma of separation from the job is not inevitable. She also shows that personal reactions to unemployment cannot be easily separated from the quality of relationships outside work. For example things tend to go worse when a marriage is not supportive and close. Other contextual factors are emphasized. Those who felt least personal control over their job loss experienced more distress; and deep, rather than causal, involvement in the job hunt process was a recipe for particular anguish if rejection occurred.

Swinburne's study has some particular parallels with the writer's own intensive investigation of 25 unemployed managers (Fineman, 1979), the study which provided the inspiration for the current one. The extent to which unemployment was experienced as traumatic, hence stressful, varied considerably in the group. Where stress did accompany unemployment one or more of the following three conditions was present: a high prior involvement in the job and a belief in one's personal competence in that job; problems which stemmed from the job circumstances coincided with others stemming from the domestic situation; repeated failures to secure a job. On the other hand some experienced little or no stress because of factors such as: seeing their predicament as a positive *opportunity* to reform their life; a very low involvement in a dissatisfying or stressful job; being able to control the unemployment decision in some way; being characteristically self-confident about their own abilities. What emerged, therefore, was a patchwork of features reflecting the personality, experience, and expectations of each manager, forming a pattern of contrasting reactions and behaviour.

Several other writers have recognized that the study of individual differences and circumstances may provide a critical key to a deeper understanding of unemployment reactions and adaptation (e.g. Hartley and Cooper, 1976; Wood, 1977; Arroba, 1979; Jahoda and Rush, 1980; Fraser, 1980; Sinfield, 1981a, b) and some lament the paucity of investigations in this direction.

Contributions from studies on blue collar unemployed

The studies on blue collar unemployed tend to fall into a similar pattern to the white collar studies. Most emphasize the trauma reaction. Blue collar work may be less 'involving' and personally committing than managerial and professional positions; however (goes the argument), it still provides the essential social, psychological, and economic framework for survival in our culture.

Without employment a person will feel deep and often lasting insecurity, loss, and helplessness (Zawadski and Lazarsfeld, 1935; Israeli, 1935; Wilcock and Franke, 1963; Sinfield, 1968; Ilfield, 1976; Parker, 1975; Strange, 1978; Leavy and Freedman, 1961; Kahn, 1964; Jenkins and Sherman, 1979). The traumatic effects can also be reflected in psychological and health deterioration (Kasl *et al.*, 1975; Cobb and Kasl, 1977).

The 1930s studies which charted the course of blue collar unemployment were the first to postulate a phase pattern to the trauma. Thus a literature review by Eisenberg and Lazarsfeld in 1938 describes a reaction series beginning with shock, progressing through to pessimism and anxiety (if there is a failure to find a new job) ending in fatalism and a 'broken attitude'. These stages have strongly influenced other researchers (e.g. Hill, 1977, 1978;

Harrison, 1976), yet with no apparent recognition of Eisenberg and Lazars-feld's important proviso:

> Of course there are large individual differences, but one would suspect that the various types of attitudes maintained are more a function of the stage of unemployment than anything else, though there is no doubt that they are also a function of the other factors that have been described above. (p. 387)

The 'other factors' described are previous economic and social status, age, sex, personality, the economic impact of the unemployment, and the length of unemployment. So we find that two of the earliest, much quoted trauma/stage advocates are in fact remarkably guarded in their conclusions, and leave plenty of room for contingencies and differences. This point has led Hyman (1979) to remark that the 'obvious' uniform, negative effects of unemployment are seductive but palpably false, and our task is to try and unravel the complex influence of social, perceptual, and cognitive factors which comprise the individual differences, a direction in which we have progressed little since the 1930s.

These sentiments are somewhat in accord with Jahoda's (1979) views on our limited advances in understanding the effects of unemployment. But while she finds sufficient recent evidence not to seriously doubt that the *overall* Eisenberg/Lazarsfeld response pattern pertains today, others are less con-vinced. For example Sinfield (1981a) musters forceful arguments against the shock-to-fatalism syndrome, describing it as part of the conventional but unproven wisdom about the impact of unemployment. The hypothesis, he contends, has been *illustrated* rather than tested and validated, with scant attention to exceptions and differences. He cites his own, and others', research experience which frequently directly contradicts the idea of a fixed pattern of responses to a psychological trauma.

The importance of the social context of unemployment has been emphasized by a number of more sociologically oriented researchers. Attachment to the work organization can vary amongst blue collar workers, as it can amongst managers and professionals. Thus those who find the rewards of an organ-ization hard to replace will feel a greater blow, come unemployment, than those less intimately attached to the system of employment (Thomas and Madigan, 1974; Martin and Fryer, 1973; Seglow, 1970; Tausky and Piedmont, 1967). The personal effects of unemployment may well spill over into, and be moderated by, the family. So existing family patterns of behaviour, health, and mutual support can be critical variables in the course and consequences of un-employment (Fagin, 1979, 1981; Ferman, 1964).

General surveys of the unemployed have usually highlighted the problems associated with economic 'deprivation'. The dramatic effects of starvation recorded in the 1930s do not appear in recent surveys (Zawadski and Lazars-feld, 1935; Daniel, 1974; Aiken *et al.*, 1968). Yet few unemployed feel adequately compensated by state financial benefits. Some analysts view the economic difficulties as *the* explanation of all the personal consequences of unemployment. So, for example, Aiken *et al.* (1968) argue that the world seems much more unfriendly when typical spending habits are severely curtailed—feelings of anomie, psychic withdrawal, and stress are the result. Loss of income means that leisure patterns are disturbed (holidays, eating out, entertaining, travelling), activities which form many individuals' social and status identities. This can lead to difficulties in maintaining family integration (Cavan, 1959).

Themes and variations—a position statement

The researches on blue and white collar unemployment mirror each other in many respects. We can view individual reactions to unemployment in terms of a gross anxiety reaction to a 'given' trauma; or, more subtly, as a series of clearly discernible phases of different reactions to that trauma; or as an idiosyncratic reaction (or reactions) to an event which is not necessarily a trauma and which is influenced by a variety of personal and contextual factors. The viewpoints vary in terms of the amount and quality of research devoted to them. The most common orientations—trauma and phases—seem more open to criticism from the existing body of research.

It would be presumptuous to claim that any one of the three major positions is the 'right' one. Each reflects certain assumptions about the nature of knowledge and understanding in social science. Thus the search for *general laws* and principles governing and explaining reactions to unemployment characterizes the trauma/phase studies: a desire to make statements such as 'the reaction to unemployment is . . .' or 'The trends suggest a general pattern of . . .'. In this type of study individual differences and contingencies are subordinated to common trends and links across people. The investigator often starts by looking for a hypothesized *trend* (or for more Popperian inspired researchers, for evidence of disconfirmation of the hypothesis). Individual exceptions to the trend are ignored or statistically dealt with as 'error variance'.

I share a view expressed by a growing nucleus of critics of traditional forms of social science that the search for generalities in this form has not been particularly helpful for our understanding. Indeed, at its extreme, it seems to take on the shape of *idée fixe*—a monomania that people, like particles in physics, or gravity, all do the same things in the same way under similar conditions. As noted earlier, 'sameness' of reaction amongst white collar unemployed is frequently more wishful thinking and statistical juggling than a reflection of what the unemployed themselves might be experiencing. Generalities based upon correlations of 0.3–0.5 and percentage 'majorities' of 50–60 leave a lot of exceptions to the 'rule'.

This is not to deny that *some* people will find unemployment a trauma, and that *some* will progress through similar kinds of phased reactions. It would be a petulant reaction to the available evidence to totally dismiss its validity. But the stance I prefer considerably elevates the status of individual differences and contingencies. It takes the position that personal reactions and adaptation to unemployment are full of different passions, and adaptations which have something to do with the variables that the more individualistically/contingent investigators have already touched upon. In particular, the *meaning* that unemployment has for the white collar worker, which is tied in with features such as his attachment to his prior employment and to employment in general, his level of control over the circumstances of his unemployment, his economic security in unemployment, his time unemployed, his 'support network', including family, friends, and professionals, his personal tolerance of anxiety and failure . . . and so on.

Thus, we *start* by assuming the possibility of many factors contributing to the *complexity* of the impact and adjustment to unemployment; that, indeed, everyone is different. If clusters and patterns then emerge, all well and good. But generality is not assumed from the start . . . differences are.

Researching in this way is a tougher, more complicated, more ambiguous route than the simpler one or two-variable model. But the potential rewards for describing and understanding a personal and social phenomenon such as unemployment should be far greater. This does not mean that we have to leap into the unemployment arena unaided. We already know (and have described) types of reactions, and factors affecting the reactions, that we might encounter. What we require now is some *individualistic* framework which will help us to tie some of these factors together in a systematic theoretical way, and which will *guide*, but not strait-jacket, our fieldwork investigation.

This framework, together with the research approach taken, forms the substance of the next chapter.

Chapter 3

Stress and Unemployment—A Framework for Analysis

My initial attempts (some 3 years ago) at analysing the varied responses of managers to unemployment utilized a psychosocial model of stress that I had been developing. This seemed to be appropriate then, as it does now, for organizing and guiding research into the impact of unemployment. Three main reasons lead to this belief:

1. The nature of the stress response has strong conceptual connections within the trauma reaction (or reaction phases). Both include experiences of chronic anxiety and tension.
2. The model was designed to capture a *range* of stress responses, psychological and physical; in particular, separating those conditions where no stress would emerge from those leading to stress.
3. The model focuses sharply on the *meaning* that a situation can have to an individual and the influence of that interpretation on the level of any subsequent stress. This includes the effect of personality variables.

Thus the model contains some of the necessary basic ingredients for exploring individual differences in reaction to unemployment. Figure 1 presents a simplified adaptation of the generic form of the model for use in the present study. The interested reader can find a fuller description in an earlier publication (Fineman, 1979).

The structure of the framework reflects the influence of a number of writers on stress—in particular Howard and Scott (1965), and Lazarus (1966). It pivots around the assumption that people will sometimes attempt to solve problems which in some way threaten their well-being. In the face of such problems they will try and do something to reduce the threat and shift towards a more comfortable, threat-free state—a condition of 'dynamic equilibrium'.

16

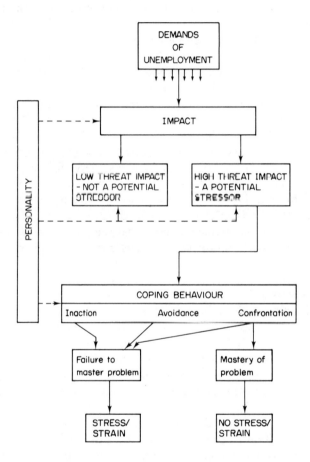

Figure 1   A Framework of the Stress Process in Unemployment

This postulate includes the recognition that human beings also receive gratification from exercising their problem-solving capacities; they will sometimes generate disequilibrium in anticipation of a future resolution to the problem so generated. They are certainly not always passive 'reactors'.

Looking at the theoretical ordering of the processes contributing to stress in Figure 1, we can envisage the operation of these princples in the unemployment context.

It is suggested, firstly, that unemployment can generate a range of possible demands, or pressures, for a person. These could be almost anything from 'How am I going to pay the bills?', to 'Where can I take that long holiday I've always promised myself?'. The *meaning* and *feelings* attached to these perceived demands constitute the quality of the *impact* of unemployment. For some people, facing such demands produces no problems—they have done it all before, or simply tend to see the bright side of things. Therefore the impact can be experienced as a fairly gentle, if not positive, happening. For others, though, the impact can be felt more severely—it all seems a very big blow. For example, there may be children's school fees to pay. There could be problems of one's status and position in life. How will the old work colleagues be replaced?

The nature of the impact of job loss depends very much on those aspects of the unemployment situation that the individual perceives as 'real' to him: what he selects into his world and what he keeps out. The magic of the human perceptual apparatus permits the creation of an infinite variety of realities—reflecting the abilities, needs, values, and shifting expectations of the perceiver. Thus, for one person, obtaining another job is seen as no problem because of his firm belief in his competence—despite the forced loss of job: 'It was the sagging market you know'. For another, getting re-employed is viewed as a considerable problem: 'If *they* didn't want me, who else will?'. Clearly, factors such as the person's attachment to his previous job, the circumstances and history of the unemployment, family cohesion and support network, and economic security are amongst the many variables which will influence these perceptions.

The experience of a *negative*, problem-laden, impact is a necessary, but not sufficient, precondition to stress in the model. Stress will only emerge if the impact is experienced as a *threat* to something that the person holds dear, *and* that threat is not effectively removed or managed.

Threat, coping, and stress

The experience of threat is accompanied by rising anxiety. Self-image or self-esteem might be at stake if the problems are not solved in some way. Also threatened could be feelings of competence, achievement, or status. The object of threat can vary considerably between people. It may be highly prized economic security to one person, but social prestige to another. Yet someone else may feel the blow even more poignantly—his carefully established personal integrity has been challenged; being unemployed is for him synonymous with personal failure.

Feeling threatened in this way is a condition of growing disequilibrium where the individual feels 'out-of-balance' compared to his lower threat, more normal state. Energy is now being mobilized to do something to reduce the threat. Three types of coping behaviour are presented in the framework—*inactivity, avoidance,* and *confrontation.* These are separated for conceptual clarity, but in practice will interlink and interact.

Inactivity and avoidance are both rather special forms of defence under threat. They are akin to classical Freudian defence mechanisms, and are usually automatic processes which protect us from acute levels of anxiety by blocking the tension build-up. Thus, someone who has been made suddenly unemployed might aimlessly drift, doing nothing in particular for weeks, avoiding the problem as much as possible. Rather different avoidant behaviour would be to become *actively* involved in anything *but* job hunting (holidays, sports, hobbies) and evading discussions about unemployment. These sorts of reactions are perhaps most likely during an early 'shock' phase of unemployment.

Inaction and avoidance may be very effective in protecting an individual from threat, but by their very nature they are mechanisms which do not deal with the specific problem. Unless somehow the problem 'goes away by itself' (for example, despite inaction, an individual is reinstated, or is offered another job) then the problem which threatens constantly lurks behind the defences. Maintaining adequate defences can be hard work, requiring a substantial drain upon available energy resources. As the person becomes more tired the defence pattern weakens, and he is in effect fighting a losing battle. He has failed to fully protect himself, and has still not directly tackled the threatening problem. The threat can now envelop him—a position of severe tension and anxiety. This painful failure situation is one of *stress.* Not only is the anxiety associated with the threat still evident, but now there is the added tension from the growing awareness of being unable to cope with threat.

So stress in our framework is a result of failure to master the threatening problems. But this failure can also come about in another way. Some unemployed people will be psychologically so equipped that the anxiety associated with the emerging threat stimulates them to tackle the problem 'head-on'. For them the best form of defence is attack. Confronting of this sort may take the form of a careful survey of the job market, exploring new job opportunities, contacting old friends, preparing a curriculum vitae, or perhaps taking up vocational training. Alternatively, it may involve the active reformulation of domestic rules—perhaps adjusting to no longer being the breadwinner and meeting threatened achievement needs through part-time work or hobbies.

If confrontation is successful, a personally effective solution to the problem is found and the threat experience is dissipated as the person returns to a state of equilibrium; stress has been avoided. 'Success' in confrontation may also be anticipatory. Thus if an individual confidently *expects* that his actions will result in a satisfactory new job, challenging new lifestyle, or whatever, in stress terms this can be psychologically equivalent to having actually experienced the good news. But there is another side to this coin. The expected outcomes of one's action might be very uncertain, or failure might be anticipated. This can induce even greater disequilibrium resulting in a chronic state of stress. An unemployed individual may constantly fail in his attempts to obtain a new job, despite a great deal of personal effort. Each successive failure can aggravate the accumulating stress, leading to feelings of hopelessness and helplessness in the face of an apparently unsolvable problem. To obtain some relief in such circumstances defence mechanisms may operate—avoidance and inaction become preferable to yet further possible failures.

The progress and characteristics of all coping attempts are influenced by an individual's more enduring personality qualities, such as self-esteem, tolerance of uncertainty, fear of failure, need to achieve, and trait anxiety. Certainly one might expect habitually anxious people to feel more vulnerable to threat than those of typically low anxiety.

Strain

A final aspect of the stress framework concerns the link with strain. Strain is used here to denote the physical reactions which can accompany stress (e.g. Levi, 1971). They have been termed 'diseases of adaptation' by Selye (1956). The list of strain reactions identified by psychosomatic researchers has lengthened over the years to provide a formidable challenge to those who insist on separating mind from body. The milder disorders identified include headaches, migraines, and back pains. More seriously we have skin complaints, diabetes, high blood pressure, ulcers, and heart disease. On this basis unemployment could feasibly result in death.

The precise nature of the link between stress and strain proves to be a bit of conundrum. One does not automatically accompany the other—they can lead relatively independent existences. Thus a person might demonstrate clear signs of strain, but not experience stress. Sometimes high anxiety is so much part and parcel of someone's life that stress is not personally recognized; yet physical changes in the body can reveal a clear pathological picture. When stress and strain are linked the time required to move from one to the other will vary between people, depending partly on the strength of experienced stress, but also on the physical resistance properties of the susceptible organs of the body.

The framework in practice: guiding principles and intervention research

The framework offers a range of possible links and hypotheses about the meaning, impact and coping strategies during unemployment. Like most attempts to bring together different parts of a complex process in a comprehensible way, a great deal remains unsaid. Thus any one of the boxes in

Figure 1 could be expanded considerably further for theoretical analysis, as could the interactions between them. The extent to which this is necessary or desirable depends on what one wishes to investigate, or know. As it stands, however, the framework encompasses a range of features which go considerably further than most existing analyses of unemployment in disentangling the *different* ways in which people might react and adapt to *their* situation. As such it can be used as an explanatory tool, or as a heuristic—a device to enable the researcher or researched to discover more.

There is a thin line between facilitating understanding and inhibiting it through the use of an *a priori* framework of this type. Although it has been developed from a considerable pool of existing theoretical and empirical data, each new group of people studied will have features of its own. Thus if one is claiming to try to understand the research *participant's* position, one's framework needs sufficient elasticity, or indeed *imprecision*, to accommodate this. Consequently the basic principles and concepts which constitute the framework have been used to form the *initial* focal elements of each research meeting, but with considerable degrees of freedom around these for capturing the participant's elaborations and personal reflections. This, of course, represents a dramatic shift in approach from traditional experimental or applied psychological research. It means that strict hypothesizing and tight, uniform questioning is not on. Such approaches make few (if any) concessions to the participants' views of what is relevant and important. So the framework has been used in low profile, in a relatively collaborative research setting; which takes us towards considering the validity of data so derived.

It would seem that one way of viewing validity is if the data generated for one's study sincerely and richly reflect the participants' perceptions, feelings, beliefs, or attitudes, rather than being ephemeral artefacts of the researcher–subject relationship, or of the measuring devices employed. There seems to be no absolute, or definitive, way that we can be sure that we are achieving validity of this sort. Yet it seems likely that the more a participant *feels* like a participant in an event that has high *face* validity for him, in which he has some genuine *choice* whether or not to take part, and from which there is some *direct, valued personal gain* (most unlikely when 'there will of course be a report of the findings published in a journal in a year or two'), then the more probable it is that validity will be achieved.

Traditionally, psychological validity of the type represented by these criteria has been swamped by technical validity—standardized procedures, pre-tested instruments, statistically rigorous sampling, and control. Ironically, the two seem often to be in contradiction. That is, the more specificity and rigour we apply to our investigation, the less room there is for getting close to, or even seeing, the world as constructed by the subject or participant. A number of writers have reached similar conclusions (e.g. Harré, 1978; Torbert, 1976; Argyris, 1980). Despite some differences between them, their studies indicate that any move towards psychological validity necessitates a special form of *interdependence* between the parties in the investigation. Indeed, inter-dependence seems to be the core feature of any study adopting a 'middle ground' position between research and consultancy (see McGivern and Fineman, 1981 for a full discussion of the various overlaps between types of research and consultancy). It means, amongst other things, that each party requires something from the other, which in turn pivots around the quality of the relationship which develops between them. This will call upon the re-searcher's interpersonal skills in a way rarely required, or desired, in traditional research.

The present study takes up the interdependence notion as the basis for an *intervention research* approach to white collar unemployment. It is through intervention research that psychological validity is, hopefully, achieved, and within which the stress framework is operationalized. The precise form of the approach taken is described next.

Chapter 4

The Intervention Research

The research approach taken was to mediate in the process of an individual's adjustment to unemployment through counselling and guidance. This role was adopted only if the individual desired such assistance and was also prepared to become involved as a research participant. Such a setting provided the potential to meet our requirements of psychological validity. Thus face validity should be high as the researcher/counsellor would, there and then, be attending to issues and problems specifically concerning the unemployed person. There was a strong possibility that the counselling process and/or advice could be *directly* useful. Furthermore, there would be no overt pressurizing or persuasion to become involved: the choice was theirs.

Basically, then, the ingredients were there for a profitable exchange. The 'contract' was that I would offer counselling and advice in return for their permission to use *this very process* for my research ends—mapping and understanding their unemployment situation. We have, therefore, a preliminary convergence of interests of the type that some writers (e.g. Friedlander, 1968) have argued comprises the foundations of 'good' research. In principle it obviates that 'thief in the night feeling' that a few traditional researchers of the unemployed have been courageous enough to declare (e.g. Maurer, 1979, p. 8); the feeling of taking much and giving little; a one-sided exchange with an individual apparently less fortunate than oneself.

Whilst the principles of the exchange could be discussed and agreed upon in advance of the actual counselling, the specific process of that event could not be so programmed. As Mangham (1982) appropriately notes (drawing upon the work of Blumer, 1969; and Hewitt, 1979) the 'rules' of many participative research interactions are likely to be fuzzy, shifting, and improvised in response to the varying interpretations and meanings attached to the interactions, *as they occur*, by the parties involved. Thus I would feel myself 'managing' the participant and myself as issues arose, and the participant would, presumably, be engaging in a similar process. I could not pre-set the precise details of my counselling, or the directions I would take. To sincerely engage with, listen to, and help my client I needed to make sense of his world from information which I could obtain only there and then. The magical property of 'trust' somehow evolved from how well I did this and the evaluation that a participant placed on my words and gestures. This process could be facilitated by the introductory contract, but prior mutual interests could not ensure that it occurred. There was much interactional work to do.

I had an agreement to 'help' and 'research', and I would make sure that they took place (suitably intermixed). They were my *raison d'être*. I would be guided by the stress framework which was always somewhere in the back of my mind. But all this occurred fairly implicitly, conversationally, and, by and large, unpredictably in emphasis and form. As the participants' issues emerged so I would develop what I saw to be the appropriate counselling/research strategy.

Client-issues affected *me*, sometimes deeply. Catalogues of failure, soul-destroying jobs, individuals I liked or disliked, their helplessness, occupations for which *I* had no affinity, marriage problems, illness . . . and so on. As a *participative* researcher, and a person, I also shared in some of their feelings and anguish. All this influenced me, and some of my specific reactions will be discussed later on. I would sometimes talk about these things with participants because it somehow felt right, for me and for them. It emerged as a natural part of the process of empathy, helping, and trust.

Types of data

Qualitative and quantitative data were collected. The former predominated, comprising the fully recorded statements made during the counselling sessions, as well as written reflections before and after the counselling. Of the follow-up data, some involved a close 'third party'–written descriptions of the unemployment experiences by a wife, husband, or friend.

Quantitative information was gathered by structured instruments before and after the counselling. It was anticipated that the qualitative and quantitative data would complement each other—each providing rather different summaries of experiences and personality.

Structured instruments, such as questionnaires and tests, are essentially predetermined and as such are manifestly rigid in a free-flowing research context. For some, they are also alienating—providing 'unreal' categories of forced response. Recognizing such, the instruments were introduced with some care and concern. The scores or patterns revealed in the questionnaires were openly discussed during a counselling session, as an intrinsic part of that session. A participant was not pressurized to complete the instruments. He was informed why they were being used, and how they *could* be useful to him and the researcher; but he was also informed about the researcher's reservations about them.

The study setting and sample

The study took place over a 4-year period—from 1976 to 1980. During that time I acted as counsellor to 100 managers and professionals attending a government-sponsored career review programme at a management training establishment.

The complete programme comprised an intensive 1- or 2-week 'package' specifically designed to help unemployed white collar workers to review themselves and their career to date, and to assist them in seeking alternative employment. The course input was broad-ranging, covering the basic skills of preparing a curriculum vitae and effective self-presentation, to sources of job information and retraining. Vocational guidance from professional counsellors and psychologists was a key element of the programme.

All course members were referred by the government's Professional and Executive Recruitment Service (PER) with whom white collar unemployed are most likely to register. Typically, a course group would comprise 12 people of wide age range, predominantly male and heterogeneous occupationally. Few arrived with any clear idea what to expect. They would stay together as a group throughout the programme. Some of the courses were residential. The physical setting was relaxing and attractive—a large country house, well furnished and well catered.

Sample characteristics

Table 1 summarizes the major descriptive characteristics of the sample in the research. This information was derived from a standard biographical question-naire which all course members completed on joining the programme, and also from the research interviews.

The age range of the predominantly male, married sample was broad—from early 20s to late 50s. The majority, however, were spread fairly evenly across the 30- to 50-year-olds. It would seem that white collar unemployment is more a mid-to-late career phenomenon amongst this group.

Unemployment does not appear to be a reflection of the 'bad employment risk'—over 70 per cent of the sample had not experienced previous unemploy-ment in their careers.

The long-term unemployed (over 1 year) were the minority in the sample; most had been out of work a short or medium period. This partly reflects PER's referral system which directs people to the programme shortly after they register with them. It also suggests that the programme was not being used as a 'dumping ground' by PER for the chronically unemployed.

The *reasons* for unemployment are perhaps the most contentious of classi-fications in Table 1, as one might expect some reluctance to reveal the known reasons for loss of job if it was seen as a personal failure or slight. Consequently the categories reported are those derived from the free content of the research

Table 1   Sample—basic characteristics (N = 100)

Age (years)		Previous unemployment	
Mean	41.89	No previous unemployment	74%
Range	21–59	Previous unemployment	26%
σ	9.10		
20s	11%	Period unemployed (months)	
30s	32%	Mean	6.55
40s	31%	Range	0–36
50s	26%	σ	8.62
		Short term (0–2 months)	41%
Sex		Medium term (3–11 months)	44%
Male	82%	Long term (12 months+)	15%
Female	18%		
		Reason for unemployment	
Marital status		Dismissed	22%
Married	65%	Compulsorily redundant	39%
Single	22%	Voluntary redundant	5%
Divorced/		Resigned/left	34%
separated	13%		

interview, and as such are probably reasonably accurate reflections of how a participant viewed his situation at that time. The largest proportion (nearly 40 per cent) described a compulsory redundancy. Typically, this was when their employing organization ceased business, 'rationalized', or was taken over by another company. This seems a fair barometer of the economic times, with particular industries collapsing completely, or dramatically reducing their size and emphasis. Few participants were given the choice to elect for redundancy—it was predominantly a take-it-or-leave-it situation. Additionally, the image of the executive's 'golden handshake' was not one that was generally portrayed in the interviews. The large pay-out was the exception rather than the rule, with a number of managers vainly pressing their ailing company for something more than the bare statutory minimum compensation.

Dismissal was described by 22 people. The stories behind these varied considerably; some of them we will touch on later. Failure to meet targets, or a personal relationship problem, was frequently a reason given. Resignation was also prompted by these situations—although factors such as feeling ill-fitted to the job, changing domestic circumstances, poor health, or an apparently attractive job offer from another company also led to resignation or leaving. Some people had worked abroad and had had to leave in a hurry during civil disturbances, or a war. Others had been on short-contract appointment abroad, and their contract had now expired. A few had retired, but had decided to return to employment.

Occupational backgrounds and qualifications

Table 2 indicates the occupations included in the sample. Managers involved at

Table 2   Sample breakdown by occupation (%)

Managers (works, general, sales, insurance, personnel, production travel, hotel, estates, office, public house, wholesale, retail)	45
Engineers/technical specialists	18
Teachers/lecturers/instructors	14
Company directors	6
Marketing/advertising/public relations	6
Banking/finance	4
Armed forces	2
Linguists	2
Social work	1
Creative design	1
Minister of religion	1
	100

all levels and different functions are represented in the largest sub-group of 45. There then follows a substantial group of professional engineers, technical specialists, and then a slightly smaller group of people engaged in various types of teaching. Together these three groups comprise 77 per cent of the sample. The remainder contains a mixed group of executives and professionals ranging from six top-level company directors, to one minister of religion.

As a group of managers and professionals their formal qualifications were, as might be expected, relatively high (Table 3). Half of the sample had some form of advanced education, 24 per cent being at degree level or above. Yet, perhaps just as noteworthy, was that 43 per cent had only basic secondary-school qualifications, or had no qualifications at all. These people were mainly to be found in various managerial positions, or in self-employment—the 'self-made' men.

Table 3   Sample breakdown by qualification (%)

Doctorate	2	
MSc/MA	4	
Degree	18	'Higher' qualifications –
Professional Diploma	15	total = 51%
Higher National Diploma	8	
Higher National Certificate	4	
'A' Level General Certificate of Education	6	
'O' Level General Certificate of Education, or equivalent	33	
No qualification	10	

The study method

Two days of each course were devoted to counselling. The course organizer informed participants of this on the first day of the course. He also informed them that I would be joining them for this activity and, if they had no objections, that some parts of this work would be for research purposes.

Prior to counselling I introduced myself to the assembled group, and directed an informal discussion on my work and on the forthcoming counselling sessions. Areas covered included our present understanding of personal reactions to unemployment, the value of counselling, and the place of relevant research. The participative nature of the counselling/research involvement was outlined, and the value and limitations of questionnaire material. By then, however, all participants had already experienced using *and* reflecting with the pencil-and-paper material they had completed for the course.

Typically, the introductory event soon turned towards the participants' own experiences of the impact of unemployment, and the variety of different positions evident amongst the group. Many would comment that they valued any event in the programme which addressed their immediate personal situation and problems. Consequently the face validity of the intervention/counselling appeared exceedingly high—no-one declined to participate.

The counselling

Counselling sessions lasted from $1\frac{1}{2}$ to 2 hours with each person. Approximately 20 per cent asked for, and received, a second meeting.

Each session began with a re-statement of the counselling and research intentions, emphasizing that we would be looking fairly closely at the circumstances which had led up to the unemployment. It was also stated that it was possible that the counselling might simply reaffirm their own action or thoughts, or it might possibly throw some new light or new angles on their position. It was difficult to state exactly what might happen.

Confidentiality issues were discussed, as were the pros and cons of using a tape-recorder. Some were initially apprehensive about tape-recording. One person did not want the recorder used. Almost invariably people very soon became 'lost' in the dynamics of the counselling process, completely forgetting about the tape-recorder—and they would spontaneously remark as much at the end of their session.

Using the stress framework

The model of stress was used to guide the discussion and to assist in the counselling postures taken. A participant was initially asked to describe what had led up to his unemployment—its history and background, including previous unemployment. From thereon the meaning and impact of the event was explored; what had been done so far, how the various demands of unemployment manifested themselves, the nature of any support received, and current views and feelings about self, unemployment, and employment.

I was self-conscious about exploring and probing areas which would cover all the basic features of the framework, but how this unfolded varied enormously. Some participants were anxious to talk about their vivid memories of the actual day of the unemployment, and the characters involved. Others soon focused on the trials and tribulations of job interviews. Still others talked of the stigma and anxiety they were experiencing, a vivid contrast to those who presented an image of optimism and even ebullience. The *dominant* direction and emphasis was determined naturally by the participant's focus of feelings. It was his unemployment, not mine. In no way would I move off an area which a person wanted to talk about until a natural plateau or full airing seemed apparent. This was also intrinsic to the cathartic value of the counselling process. Furthermore, revelations of this intensity were probably the very best research data I could obtain in these circumstances. The content could be replete with potential for inference concerning impact, personality, threat, stress, and so on.

My overall counselling objective (as far as I could state one) was to assist the client in moving in the direction or directions he desired. Some people had no clear directions, but wanted some. So this became one of the main problems to address during the counselling. The range of problems and difficulties presented was considerable, and could shift in emphasis during the counselling. They included managing current anxieties and feelings of inadequacy and failure; deciding upon changes in direction of career; adjusting to lack of regular, future employment; choosing among several available and equally attractive jobs; breaking out of feelings of paralysis and inertia; how to tackle the job market; how to present oneself at job interviews; and explaining to potential employers that 'unemployed does not mean incompetent'.

It was soon apparent that certain participants were feeling highly stressed, and some of them described symptoms of strain. In such cases the threatening problems, reasons for threat, and coping methods used became a focal part of the counselling analysis. For example, some people were clearly avoiding turning towards the job market because of the pain and hurt that was preoccupying them. The appropriate counselling role here seemed to be as an 'empathetic ear' whereby individuals could begin to unload some of their burden. If they began to feel a little lighter then more confronting strategies could be discussed. It was not untypical in such circumstances that the blackness of the unemployment event coloured all aspects of life and self.

Ways of solving the problem of actually getting a job occupied many discussions. Some would persevere along a familiar, but now overtrodden route, constantly failing to get anywhere. New possible avenues were explored in the light of their various abilities and aspirations. Retraining and further education were sometimes considered. For many, the automatic reaction to unemployment was to seek a job similar to the previous one—the comfort of the familiar, or 'better the devil you know'. This could be a desperate position in a job market where very few such jobs still existed. So it became one of the most challenging of the counselling tasks to try and assist people towards viewing themselves in a different way for an alternative job or career.

The stress framework was helpful in locating precise intervention points during counselling, while automatically ensuring comprehensive coverage of the variables of interest in the research. Yet, as previously emphasized, each participant provided his own direction, adding the essential dramatic narrative to bring to life the abstractedness of the framework.

It is difficult to know precisely how one should determine the success or otherwise of a counselling venture such as this. Were the participants helped? Certainly, many said positive things, such as 'I feel much better now', 'I never thought of that; I'll try it', 'You've given me something positive to do at last', 'I had a feeling that I shouldn't go back into that type of work; our discussions have confirmed this', 'Thanks, you've helped me—but I can't pinpoint where or how!'

In most of these cases I *felt* that the counselling had helped—that something had 'clicked'. I had offered, or the participant had discovered, some novel perspective—a way out of a situation which initially looked intractable. But not all cases felt so good. Sometimes a participant had, apparently, done everything he could do, and no new avenues seemed appropriate or possible. As a counsellor I could sometimes help the client towards accepting this and assist him in seeking ways of managing his disappointment or stress. Other times I could not. The sense of hopelessness and helplessness was too deep and chronic to be alleviated in one or two counselling sessions. I would suggest other people or agencies who might be able to help on a longer-term basis, and this would often leave *me* with feelings of helplessness. Part of me would recognize that their difficulties were beyond the reach of my skills, or perhaps outside the scope of any counselling intervention. But another part of me was keen to 'give' something plausible and tangible to each client—some immediate contribution towards solving their unemployment problems. Logically, of course, referring them to someone else more suited to their needs did just this. It was the 'responsible', 'professional' thing to do. Nevertheless, emotionally, it felt like a cop-out; as if I were reneging on our contract. Somehow the nature of our mutual ties implied that they required something more from me than a response which looked similar to that which they receive from the bureaucrats of unemployment. I gained some solace from the belief that they would view my advice or suggestions differently, as they were the product of a rather special relationship. However, the aftertaste that lingered was that maybe I *was* a 'thief in the night'. I was the employed, professional researcher/helper and I had taken from them more than I could return.

That extra fillip or direction that counselling can provide was a powerful motivator for some people. There is evidence from the follow-up to the course that it broke through their despair or dejection to give them enough hope and energy to do more things for themselves and finally to gain a satisfactory job. Others did not fare so well. Their profound loneliness and vulnerability before and during counselling suggested that continuing support would be essential to maintain any assisted rise in self-confidence and optimism.

The structured instruments

The measuring instruments employed examined three main areas pertinent to the impact of and reactions to unemployment: stress, strain, and self-esteem. Each of these was tapped qualitatively through the counselling interviews, however the more standardized measurement provided rather different, complementary information. They were normally filled in shortly before the counselling sessions.

Stress. The General Health Questionnaire devised by Goldberg (1972) was used to measure stress. This instrument is impressive for its careful construction and validation, and it is one that has proved helpful in my previous analyses of the reactions of the unemployed. The version used contained 30 items each consisting of a question asking whether the respondent has, over the past few weeks, experienced a particular symptom or behaviour on a scale ranging from 'less than usual' to 'much more than usual'. The items refer to typical stress reactions, such as anxiety, depression, and feelings of social inadequacy. The possible scores on the questionnaire range from zero to 30 (maximum stress).

Strain. A checklist of 18 strain signs and symptoms was drawn up. These were culled from the general literature on psychosomatic illness and the physical concomitants of stress. The list covered complaints such as skin ailments, asthma, heart problems, stomach upsets, diabetes, high blood pressure, and difficulty in breathing. The questionnaire asked respondents to indicate against each complaint whether or not they had been troubled in that way since their unemployment and to say whether or not they had been previously troubled by such a complaint. Thus a distinction could be drawn between strain which was apparently specifically associated with the unemployment, and strain which was possibly a continuation of a pre-existing chronic condition. The strain questionnaire is reproduced in Appendix A. The maximum strain score is 18, one point being assigned to each symptom checked.

Self-esteem. What emerges from many of the studies on the impact of unemployment is that the 'self' can get quite a battering. Feeling inferior, losing self-respect, reducing self-confidence, and damaging the ego are amongst the various expressions of this. Implicit in the arguments concerning the effects of unemployment on the self is that one's self-*evaluation*, or self-*esteem*, is vulnerable and changeable under certain circumstances. This assumption is also reflected in some of the literature on the effects of stress on self-esteem (e.g. Jaco, 1970; Helmreich, 1972). In the present study we shall assume that overall feelings about oneself can be linked with the experiences of unemployment, in that the job and the self may become inextricably intermingled.

The measure of global self-esteem used in this study was a 10-item scale developed by Rosenberg (1965). It asks for the respondent's level of agreement with self-descriptive statements such as 'I feel I do not have much to be proud of', and 'At times I think I am no good at all'. Each relates to present feelings. The scale's apparent simplicity belies its technical sophistication. Rosenberg has carefully checked for unidimensionality, reliability, and validity, as well as attending to its ease and economy of administration, and face validity. He derives six subscales from the items. In this study the lowest self-esteem score is zero, and the highest six.

Other measures

In addition to the stress, strain, and self-esteem measures, it was possible to have access to the standard data recorded by each participant on joining the programme. As well as biographical information some of the sample completed the Eysenck Personality Inventory (EPI) (Eysenck and Eysenck, 1964). The EPI score in which I was particularly interested concerned trait anxiety. This refers to an individual's customary predisposition to feel anxious; his characteristic threshold for experiencing tension. One would expect that the level of trait anxiety could influence (a) the nature of the impact of job loss, (b) whether or not the problems are perceived as threatening, and (c) the type of coping behaviours engaged. For example, the highly anxious person may be more likely to be disturbed by his unemployment and less able to coolly confront his problems and job search.

Before and after measures

One convenience of standardized measures is that they can be readily used to detect certain limited, specific changes over time. Consequently the measures of stress, strain, and self-esteem were also included in a follow-up questionnaire administered 6 months after completion of the course. I was curious about a number of possible shifts over time. For example: Does stress and strain decline, and self-esteem improve if a person becomes employed? Or does it depend on the type of job obtained? Do those people who initially feel positive and unthreatened by their unemployment (low stress and strain, high self-esteem) remain so after a further 6 months unemployment? Or are the effects of continuing unemployment uniformly erosive and destructive? The test scores could be used to explore these possible changes, but, once again, it was felt that the 'guts' of the experience could only be fully portrayed if the respondent was allowed to do so freely in his own terms. Unfortunately it was not possible for me personally to visit each participant for this purpose. Second best was a mailed questionnaire containing (together with the tests) the following general questions:

1. Since we last saw you what, if anything, have you managed to *do* to find a job? (Where did you go? How did you go about it? What were the difficulties? What were your feelings about the process?)
2. How has your life in general been affected? (Influence on family, friends, etc. Please cite relevant experiences.)
3. What moral support, if any, have you had from other people? (What characterizes their support? Who has it come from? Has it been sufficient?)
4. What is it like having 'unemployed' status? (How does it affect the way you see yourself and the way others see you?)
5. Any other comments?

Each of these questions was typed at the top of a blank page, providing plenty of space for comment. The general nature of this follow-up was discussed during the course and it was accompanied by a personal letter. After two reminders a total of 72 per cent of questionnaires were returned. All were usable in the analysis, although not all were complete. A few people chose to write a personal letter instead of returning the questionnaire; some attached a letter to the completed questionnaire.

The viewpoint of others

As is evident from our earlier review of the literature, unemployment can spill over into many spheres of one's life, involving family or friends, sometimes in ways quite unfamiliar and problematic for them. What is it like for 'significant' other people who have to live through, or share, unemployment? How do *they* see the problems and adjustments that arise, and what effect does it have on them?

In the follow-up each person was asked if they would hand over a special part of the questionnaire to another person to fill in. This was intimated in the following manner:

It would be very valuable if we could obtain some opinions on your predicament from someone who knows you well and who has 'lived with you' through your experiences.

If you have no objection, and if it is convenient, please could you *separate* this sheet from the rest and pass it to your wife, husband, close friend, or someone else who has been near to you during your unemployment. Do discuss this person's opinions with him or her after they have been recorded.

What relationship is this person to you?

To the other person:
As you have seen the influence of unemployment on the individual who has handed you this sheet, please could you give us your observations? For example, what has it looked like from your side of the fence? What have been the worst and best periods? What roles have you played? How has it affected you? Please elaborate as much as possible.

This rather unusual approach was asking quite a lot of participants, so I was fairly conservative in my expectations. Up until this point our exchanges had been on a one-to-one basis, involving no other person. Indeed, it was not uncommon for a participant to see his problem as very much *his* own, to the relative exclusion of his close family or friends.

I received 22 returns on this part of the questionnaire, mainly from wives, but also from friends, fiancées, and one vicar. Together they provide a revealing alternative perspective on the impact of unemployment. They are fully discussed in Chapter 9. Six participants gave reasons for not handing over this part to someone else. They ranged from fairly cursory statements such as 'My wife sees it like I do', to more poignant ones such as 'It's too painful to go over this again with my wife; it's like rubbing salt into the wound'.

Analysing the data

The information collected from the study was analysed and synthesized in a variety of different ways.

Qualitative data. The tape-recordings of the counselling interviews were replayed, during which time an initial content analysis was made. Primary focus was on the *meaning* and *consequences* of unemployment to each person. Any patterns and clusters which were then apparent formed the major format of this part of the initial results. However, the individual differences within and between clusters were retained (in statement form) to maximize the descriptive richness of the data. There then followed a re-analysis of the qualitative data to examine the nature and range of stress responses. Consequently the categorization followed the conceptual categories outlined in the stress framework.

The follow-up questionnaire provided a further source of qualitative data. Comments from participants and their 'significant others' were analysed according to areas such as the longer-term impact of unemployment, the effect on one's life and family, perceptions of status, and the nature of support received. The differences between three main sub-groups were examined; those who were still unemployed, those who were satisfactorily employed, and those who were unsatisfactorily employed.

Quantitative data. The scores on the various tests provided additional vehicles for interpreting the qualitative results concerning the impact of unemployment, and changes over time, as well as linking in to specific points on the stress model. The sample of 100 was susceptible to various forms of statistical analyses for group and sub-group trends. Summary details are presented in the results which follow, and a full-sample analysis in Chapter 12.

Chapter 5

The Impact of Unemployment

We begin by looking at the way unemployment presented itself to the participants. The meaning it had, the initial demands it made of them, and the problems it created for them.

It was readily apparent from the interviews that formal employment provided a pattern activity so deeply ingrained that its absence invariably resulted in a fundamental psychological reaction. The nature of this reaction was, however, far from uniform. The participants varied in the strength and form of attachment to their jobs; consequently job loss meant different things to different people.

Three broad categories of impact were discernible. Those feeling a profound *rejection or failure* (42 per cent); those feeling they had *lost something of particular value* (23 per cent); and those seeing their predicament as an *acceptable, if not positive experience* (35 per cent). These categories are based upon the *dominant* expressions portrayed in the interviews, but they are not necessarily mutually exclusive. So some people felt a profound rejection and (less dominantly) a feeling of loss. Others could express positive feelings and also declare that they felt rejected. Let us examine the impact categories and their dimensions more closely. The reports which follow, like all that appear in this book, have been modified in certain places (for example, people's names and company affiliations) to protect confidentiality.

Rejection and failure

Brian, General Sales Manager, age 46

In hindsight it was a bad move when I took my last job. I had a General Manager who wouldn't let me do a true General Sales Manager's job. The honeymoon period over the last 2 or 3 years ended with the recession. The General Manager started to tighten up. Finally there was an incident when I

36

wanted to send a letter to one of my managers to warn him that he had been taking time off without permission. The Managing Director agreed with me, so I did it. Then the manager contested *my* loyalty to the company in retort! The Managing Director asked us both to put in reports on the matter.

Well, one afternoon I was called into his office. He said he'd made a decision—I was the one to go. It would make the biggest financial saving. What a shock! I was shattered. Now, at the age of 46 I've got to get up and start all over again. And what kind of company hives off its General Sales Manager? I certainly didn't link the company's misfortunes with *me* personally. I couldn't really find out the grounds on which I had been finished. What am I to do now—return to a failing industry? Where did *I* go wrong?

Phillip, Marketing Manager, age 44

The company had given me a really super offer to join them—one I couldn't refuse. The billing for their clients was in the six-figure mark. I enjoyed the job very much—but it became very demanding physically, especially after I found I needed a cartilage operation.

Then the disaster. I returned from a two-week holiday to be told that my services were no longer required on account of upsetting a member of the client organization. This was absolutely shattering! I had tried to complete my workload before leaving the office, and I had no doubts in my mind that there would be a position to return to. The blow gave me considerable worry—I was in a state of shock because it all happened so quickly.

I felt even worse when my 7-year-old daughter said 'Why don't they need you daddy?' She couldn't comprehend what had happened after an enjoyable holiday—and neither could I.

Ron, Chief Engineer, age 56

I *never* considered I'd be out of work. I was really shocked when I learned I'd have to go. The more people sympathized with me the worse it got. I went out with a bang! Had a big office party. People asked me why I was celebrating. I said 'I'm not—but if I sat here crying you'd wonder what the hell was the matter with me!'

I felt very resentful at first and wanted to get my own back. I was there 14 years and most of this period I enjoyed my job. The company gradually shrank from 120 people to around 40. Most of my job dried up as investment dried up. Things became a bit traumatic for me. Younger people with different qualifications to mine were brought in—rather cheaper than me! Now the company has been bought up with a young, qualified engineer in my place. I've been trying virtually everything to recover my self-respect and status—but I feel people just walk over me. Yes, I'm feeling bitterly disappointed. My wife says I'm obviously worried. But it's not as bad as those last months in the company when the uncertainty was excruciating. I couldn't sleep at night. Got sleeping tablets from the doctor.

Mick, Managing Director, age 57

My career developed from general management to consultancy to Directorship of a multinational oil company. I was Managing Director for 5 years. Success stories, high politics, and intrigue. It was enormous fun which landed me *fantastic* bonuses as profits soared. I made the company a market leader. But the team spirit was broken up with the fragmenting of the company. Success breeds jealousy. Eventually I got the sack by the Chairman. This has been *the* traumatic event of my career. Now life has begun to claim its accumulated debts.

I'm left with little. There's no work for me as a consultant—and anything I do is pathetic compared with the hurly burly of industry. I've speculated, but disastrously. I now drink more, scan the newspapers, and spin out the day. It's bloody hell. I'm really back where I was 10 years ago, but several thousand pounds worse off. I've had to give up my house. I could have a premature heart attack; it's in the family. But I'd rather go out in full flood than muck about in the shallows.

Edward, Sales Manager, age 35

I was in up-market microprocessing equipment. I was given a regional office to run and just pitched into the deep end with no training. I just sank. I couldn't possibly meet their speed of sales in a cold territory. They really wanted me to have a complete killer instinct. I was to knock out three or four people in the middle management of a client organization and get right to the top. Chew people up and spit them out. This isn't me.

But the firm gave me *nothing* in terms of support. The General Manager refused to see me. It was a hire-and-fire outfit. I guess it *was* partly my fault though, and it was pretty traumatic for me. A real rejection. It was awful for my family as well. My wife is fairly pessimistic which I find very demoralizing.

Feelings of failure, humiliation, and rejection come through these accounts. The loss of jobs has triggered various doubts—particularly about personal competence and confidence. What hits hard is the insecurity and feeling tainted in some way. Others put their key comments in similar ways:

I was accused of incompetence; it destroyed my confidence. I now feel that I can't complete anything.

I feel humiliated, drained in confidence. They 'let me go' with no reason given.

I failed at my job, and my confidence is now completely shattered. I *don't* want another failure.

I *thought* I'd found security. Now I feel rejected, lonely, and wonder about my confidence.

I felt dirty after being fired. I failed—it was my fault basically.

Many of these people describe the shock of a taken-for-granted world being suddenly turned upside-down: as if being propelled into a vacuum and left floating helplessly. Even those who knew what was coming, observing the ranks closing against them, or the redundancy plans gradually emerging, were no less stunned by the experience. All of these individuals were most likely to talk of the shock of the event. The self had been severely assaulted.

But feelings of inadequacy were not always associated with the specific job loss. The impact of the immediate *aftermath* was sometimes remembered as the most difficult period:

Cyril, Finance Manager, age 46
I was made redundant along with 360 others. I saw it coming, but was assured it wouldn't hit me. Nevertheless I was completely disillusioned with senior management. The Managing Director used to go out to the local pub at 12 noon and return at 3 p.m., absolutely paralytic. Another one washes his car and the third would lock himself in his room. You begin to think you're wasting your time.

So I resigned myself to redundancy and was happy to leave. I thought I'd get my house in order and then get a job. But it hasn't worked out like this. I've run into deep financial problems which have pushed me into tranquillizers. I've become very worried about spending my money with little coming in. I haven't told many people that I'm unemployed. Should I go back into finance? Or change my past completely? Self employable? I'm beginning to think I've wasted my life up to date and unless I do something now I'll never do anything.

Michael, Administrative Manager, age 40
The political upheaval in Eastern Europe meant a premature ending of my contract, so back I came to the UK. I didn't mind too much because I really felt I'd have no problems getting a job. Previously I'd seen an advertisement, applied for the job and got it. So initially I simply approached contacts. But these came to nothing. I then realized I'd have to take it all rather more seriously.

I'm a fairly placid person, but it's now beginning to get to me. The money side is worrying me. I've made so many direct approaches to companies and only a very few respond to the application forms. In 3 months I've got nowhere. After approaching lots of companies the word can get round—so what's wrong with this guy? I'm not at a dead end yet—but if I take a step sideways or backwards, where would I be then?

Dave, Managing Director, age 43

Basically I had to close down my engineering business—there was nothing else I could do in the declining market. I don't feel too bad about it as I got a lot out of it. It had to happen. Nevertheless, it *is* a failure and I don't want to repeat it!

What *has* come as a shock, however, is the realization that I *don't* know what job to seek. Also, I can find no niche at home. I've tried hard to help with things around the house that I couldn't do for my wife while I was at work—and I'm seen as a nuisance. I'm in the way. I feel rejected and no-one knows where they stand.

The early days of unemployment were distressing for these individuals, often confounding their expectations. Some participants would bounce into the job market with faith and hope—but receive little charity in return. They soon found that they could expend masses of energy researching and exploring the market, preparing CVs, filling in application forms, and even knocking on doors—to see no tangible results at the end. The feelings of rejection and failure could lead to depression and hopelessness. The 'system' seemed impenetrable. Their pride soon turned to humiliation, cynicism, and distress. Characteristic comments were:

I'm now bitter and desperate. I keep applying, keep dropping my aspirations, and keep failing.

I feel spiritually decimated. I left my job to retrain as a teacher and now I'm qualified no-one wants me. Am I any good at all?

I haven't had a single job offer—I really feel the system is against me.

So many false promises from prospective employers erode one's confidence.

The utter blow is to have failed a trade test in something which has been my profession for 27 years! What's my experience worth?

Loss

Twenty-three of the participants described the impact of their unemployment in terms of the loss of something particularly valued. Their sentiments did not have quite the poignance or intensity of the previous group. Nor were they as profound as would be expected from the loss of a loved one (a reaction suggested by some unemployment researchers). It was more a general sense of sadness, weariness, and regret, perhaps tinged with reproach.

For some, the loss was focused on the job itself and the energy put into creating and maintaining it. This seems a particularly 'managerial and professional' loss. For example:

Len, General Manager, age 44

I was approached by the company to join and then was told there would be no problem about cash—that was two years ago. Then, in the first 4 months a bank statement showed me I was £15,000 overdrawn. Nevertheless I pulled the company round from nothing to £100,000 turnover—which I thought was quite good.

Then, just a month ago the Managing Director (my personal friend!) informs me that the overall organization was in trouble and my operation would have to go. My God! The most unpalatable thing is, having worked so hard to build it up, and then have to dismantle my own product! All that effort gone. What a waste! I can't disguise occasional feelings of rancour about the whole thing.

Rod, Catering Manager, age 35

My boss asked me if I would accept redundancy payment as he could operate without me. I felt *really* piqued. It was a small, very profitable organization with five restaurants—we could have gone a long way together. But I took redundancy because I was angry and felt I deserved a break. I was overworked by the organization. I hadn't had 4 complete days off in 2 years. After I'd built up one restaurant I was shifted on to another. It was a catalogue of broken promises, and I had become exhausted and ill.

But, for all this, I found it a big tear to leave. Having built it all up, devoted my skills to making it something, I do miss it now. I wish I were back.

Graham, Audit Manager, age 36

The company approached me to sort out their stock. I was very flattered by the offer. After 2 weeks I found that the department was in a bigger mess than I thought. It would take a while to sort out. Many operations hinged around my work—sales, workshops, production. I was being pressed very hard by other managers to get things straight. So I pulled out all of the stops. I was spending 14–15 hours at the office, working at home as well. I even persuaded sub-contractors to delay their accounts to us. It was all coming together well when I was asked to resign. One sales manager wasn't happy about his sales and he blamed my operation. They wanted the results in 3 months—which needed a full financial year!

I was *sickened* and disheartened. All that work for someone else to reap the benefit and cream. My sacrifice had been enormous, having also had to cope with a new baby at home.

Arthur, Managing Director, age 45

Trade became terrible in the textile industry, but we could just about hold our own—until inflation overtook us. We couldn't cope with it so we sold out. We had absolutely no choice. The big boys can weather the storms in ways in which the smaller fry cannot.

I was so upset when the company folded after all the work I'd put into it. It really makes me cry. The company we sold to is now making lots of money—out of all my work!

A picture is presented of the loss of something that was an extension of oneself, carefully built up and nurtured, perhaps reflecting years of effort. Some talked of the absolute finality of their job loss. No other job could effectively replace something which was so firmly 'right' for them. Somehow they felt robbed of what was appropriately theirs. Yet such task engagement did not characterise all of this group. The ache, for some, was more for the people with whom they had worked. For example:

Brian, Supplies Manager, age 33
We'd been living under a cloud for 4 months. Everybody felt pretty sick about it as nobody knew whether or not they would have a job. We sat there doing nothing. We kept sane by fantasizing about our futures. But also *seriously* planning what we could do *together* when we were out of the place.

It was then a real shock for me to find out that, finally, I was the only one of my group who had gone! I waited for my colleagues to join me and work on the plans we had made but no-one came. I was really alone. This, perhaps, was the worst element of all.

Richard, Sales Director, age 57
I worked 29 years for the company—aeronautics. During this period I had various roles ranging from the General Manager of the Division to Sales Director. But things went wrong. The travel and commuting was enormously demanding, and I was gradually edged out by the Managing Director. My job was impoverished. It lost its scope and satisfaction.

So I took early retirement. It was my decision. But when my retirement day came I realized I had done completely the wrong thing. I had all my good colleagues around me saying goodbye. It was shattering. *Then* I knew I shouldn't be retiring. *They* were the reason I should have stayed on. I now realize that it's better to be in the imperfect job than in no job at all.

There was one final group here whose loss could be characterized in more global terms—a large chunk of their lives had simply disappeared.

Annie, Lecturer, age 50
Before the college was closed down I thought it would be rather exciting to be kicked out. A tantalizing prospect—a frissant. A new challenge in life! But now I so long to be back. I *really* miss the political cut-and-thrust of college life—the struggles, manoeuvrings, and power plays. I'm getting bored. I'd love to get back to the job—I loved it.

I feel reasonably secure, but I'm beginning to worry about money.

Inflation concerns me. I'm getting stomach-upsets, headaches and back-aches—things I've never had before.

Harry, Works Director, age 55
I carried through a £3 million re-equipment and reorganization of the engineering works. But this was borrowed money. So with sharp increases in interest rates, plus the recession, we couldn't carry on. It was punch after punch—VAT, oil prices. Cutbacks everywhere.

Then suddenly the Managing Director gave me a fortnight's notice. I was shattered. Especially after relocating for the job, for which my wife had to give up her full-time job. But what really hit me, after about 10 days, was the sudden shift from high activity to low activity. I was itching to do something but there was nowhere to apply my energy. My way of life had gone.

There was a particularly deep void for those who had committed many years to their last job—'Twenty-four years—a damn big part of your life just gone'. 'After 28 years in an enjoyable job, what on earth can replace it?' 'It was so *central* to my life, for so long.'

Loss, then, has several distinct dimensions—like the experience of rejection and failure. This differentiated pattern also occurs with those experiencing reactions quite contrary to these. Let us look at this group.

Acceptable and positive reactions

Those comprising this, the second-largest, group (over one-third of the participants) showed no signs of trauma or shock. Unemployment for them was an acceptable, if not enjoyable, event. Unlike those who felt they had failed after an optimistic start in the job market, this group's basic optimism transcended any difficulties they had had in the job market. Several factors contributed to these reactions.

Many had felt trapped in an unsatisfactory or stressful job from which they basically longed to be free—unemployment offered a welcome way out:

Ray, Industrial Relations Manager, age 42
I was working too hard. I'd stopped communicating with my family. Phone calls on industrial relations at midnight. I had to lower my arguments to a base level at all times—it was degrading. Coupled with this I found that the Managing Director was steadily taking more and more of my territory—carefully planned moves, never showing his cards.

So I declared that I'd had enough. Unless I had more freedom and discretion I would resign—which is what I did. I've felt great! No regrets at all at leaving all this. I did what I *wanted* to do. Now I don't want to make a decision too quickly and sell myself short.

Helen, Management Trainee, age 21

I got into this highly prestigious retailing organization as a trainee. Generally speaking I *loved* working with the people, but *hated* the job. I got bogged down with rules and regulations. I didn't know where to put stock. There was no room for initiative—it was all dictated by Head Office.

For ages I didn't know what to replace the job with. I felt trapped, numb. I couldn't listen to what people were saying. I was gaining nothing. I was ripped off so many times that I couldn't stand up for myself—I was terrified. But it was a 'good job' with a 'good company'. I cared what people thought so I didn't want to be unemployed.

Suddenly I came to terms with it and gave in my notice. I met a chap who helped to stick me back together. I felt *terrific* the day I left. And now I feel on cloud nine! It's amazing what that job did to me! It stopped me—even regressed me.

Alex, General Manager, age 54

It was a great sense of relief to leave. It was *terrible* going to work there. I've never experienced so much stress in my life. I felt awful going to work in the morning, and that's *never* been me! If anything I've been a workaholic— *loved* work!

I had a series of rows. I increased sales, which I felt very proud of. I then got a warning letter out of the blue after a row in the board room. The letter told me to increase productivity to a ridiculous amount. I got thoroughly despondent with the whole setup. I may have been a little outspoken, but I thought that this was my responsibility. And I finished up out of work.

Apart from the relief of it all, it has galvanized me to get on with job hunting—something new.

The deep influence of a stultifying, or entrapping, job pervades these reactions. Others talk of 'release from a vacuum', 'an enormous weight off my shoulders', 'a cleansing period for me', 'lost my lethargy—I'm alive', 'free at last!'. The relief seemed all the greater if there had been a long period of disaffection, or prolonged uncertainty before a definite decision on job loss (by the job-holder or employer).

The joy of 'escaping' frequently turned into firm optimism, and even joy, at the prospect of a different future.

Rick, General Manager, age 50

The lease expired of the premises where we worked. I was led to believe that I'd be employed elsewhere. But I didn't really believe this—and I was right!

During the last year or two I've had a lot of pressures at work, and at home. They were really hard-down on you, demanding higher and higher targets—never satisfied.

After I left I thought 'Thank God—I'm a happy man!' At the same time I solved my home problems. So it made me take stock of myself and re-appraise. I'm now more hopeful than I've been for a long time. I'm much more confident in myself. I've sought new qualifications—I've wanted to *learn*.

Barry, Production Supervisor, age 49

I've been with the company for 13 years—worked my way up. In recent years it's all become *so* monotonous and predictable. It's mass production, so we were always facing discipline problems and union haggles. It really got me down. There was little respect from other people. The atmosphere has been awful. I've tried not to take it home but my wife could see it in me. I became very irritable. I wasn't happy.

Well, the redundancy helped me to make up my mind to leave! I missed some of my old mates to start with, but otherwise it was a tremendous relief. It was an unbearable job. Now I can do what I've always wanted to do—run a shop! I'm setting it all up now. It's great!

Job loss seemed to signal a 're-birth' to these people. Participants talked of 'a new beginning', 'search for a new life purpose', and 'reassessing the direction of life'.

A few were more low-keyed and philosophical about their predicament; it was all part of the inevitable pattern of things:

I accept that I'll never really adequately replace the job. That's life.

It was an economic necessity for the company; no ill feelings. It's much worse for others.

No-one owes me a living. I'm an optimist—as one door closes another opens.

It's happened to me before. I feel optimistic and philosophical.

Perhaps the most forceful image one receives from these accounts is that of a large proportion of the group being so glad to have left their jobs. It is hard to believe that this reflects some gross rationalization process; the statements were cross-validated in different ways at various points in the counselling process. So the naive stereotype of the privileged white collar worker enjoying a challenging job, as well as an excellent salary and working conditions, does not fit too well with these data. Managers and professionals can be trapped in inappropriate jobs like any other occupational group. Indeed, one might speculate that when they are feeling trapped the teeth of the trap bite deeper than in other jobs. For example, there are the mortgage commitments tied in with a regular salary, the built-up progression to promotion and the non-transferability of certain key, highly specialized, skills. Yet when the shackles are released the predominant reaction (apart from the relief of it all) is to meet

46

frustrated needs for achievement and self-actualization. It is the *intrinsic* nature of the potential new job which is immediately emphasized, not the salary and conditions which formed part of the old entrapping web.

Why different forms of impact?

What is it that leads these people to see unemployment in such markedly different ways? The qualitative data have already provided some hints in this direction. Rejection and failure is closely tied in with some people's sensitivity and vulnerability to an implicit or explicit personal rejection. The overall image of their competence in life was tied in with competence in the job. To be made unemployed signified a dramatic vote of 'no confidence'. Their personal recognition and security stemmed dominantly from the job, and this was suddenly vitiated with the unemployment. Characteristically these people could not envisage any alternative source of recognition and security other *than* their jobs.

Some did not experience rejection and failure immediately because they could maintain their identity and feelings of competence by 'working' at job seeking. So any early feelings of rejection were overtaken by the challenge and activity of looking for a new job. But this activity was soon to become singularly lacking in reward. They were now constantly being rejected—by prospective employers' refusal letters, disheartening interviews, and unfulfilled promises by friends, colleagues, and contacts. Indeed, they would frequently remark how fast an apparently well-established support network could dissolve. No-one wanted to know them.

Feelings of loss can be rather differently explained. Whereas rejection and failure stemmed from a deep hurt to a sensitive core aspect of self-image, the loss was rather more distanced from these central features of personality. Unemployment was not viewed as a *judgement* on oneself, but as a loss of something closely *associated* with oneself. 'The job was everything *to* me, but it wasn't *all* me' is the type of phrase which captures this notion. What each person identified as losing varied. Most lost a big personal investment. Masses of time and energy devoted to building and creating something (a business, a product, or a process) they no longer belonged to or owned. Others lost associates whom they valued even more than the specific job or task. But for some the loss was a combination of these, and more—a way of life had gone.

The bond between the individual and his job was very different for those who experienced the unemployment as an acceptable or positive event. A few saw their work as 'just another job', so its loss was of no great upset. Other spheres of their lives were usually balanced with their jobs— so leisure interests, hobbies, and other paid work (such as consultancy, or a part-time business) would play an important role in meeting their needs. These activities still existed after the 'main' job had gone. But particularly striking was how alienated most had felt in their previous jobs. Although they went through the 'motions' of work, the rewards had long since disappeared. Many had grown out of their jobs. What was once challenging provided a challenge no more and they could find no opportunity to change the situation. Some who had 'succeeded' by moving up the promotional ladder found that they had no head for heights after all. The experienced demands of the senior position were far less satisfying than those of the more junior post: more paperwork, less contact with the 'front line', unpalatable politicking, and industrial relations pressures. Given these sorts of situations it is not surprising that unemployment should feel like a ray of bright light. What seemed a trap was now an open door. What was a hopeless, inextricable predicament had now been replaced by one that had lots of exciting promise. Old aspirations and dreams were rekindled.

We can say a little more about the variability in impact by looking at some of the background variables in the study (see Appendix B).

Stress, strain, and self-esteem. There are clear hints in the qualitative data that stress, strain, and self-esteem are directly influenced by the way a participant defines the impact of his job loss. This is corroborated statistically (Appendix Table B1). There is a definite trend suggesting that when impact is defined as a rejection or failure, stress and strain are at their highest, and self-esteem at its lowest. Conversely, those who view their unemployment in acceptable or positive terms are least inclined to report high stress, high strain, or low esteem.

Anxiety. How people see their predicament will mirror their personalities in some way (see Figure 1) as will the nature of their relationship with their job. So, for example, the perpetual optimist is likely to 'see' his unemployment as less devastating than the habitual pessimist. The principle should operate analogously for trait anxiety. Thus the more characteristically anxious participant ought to be found amongst those experiencing the impact of their job loss in negative, worrying terms. The analysis of the part of the group that completed the EPI accords with this expectation (Table B2). Those describing rejection, failure, or loss have a significantly higher anxiety score than those experiencing the event more positively.

Reason for unemployment. The way an individual parted company from his organization does not generally contribute to the overall impact of the unemployment. The prior relationship he had with the job, and his early experiences in the job market, are likely to be better touchstones in this respect. However, looking more closely into the data (Table B3), one is struck by the relatively large proportion of reject/failure people who were either dismissed or made compulsorily redundant, with a comparatively smaller trend in the same direction for those experiencing loss. Statistically insignificant maybe;

experientially though, there is no doubt that some found being 'forced out' exceedingly distressing, and their overall feeling of rejection, failure, or loss was very much mixed up with these memories of the parting. This, of course, also applies to positive feelings. So a 'bad' departure could lead to enhanced feelings of relief at 'getting out'.

The accounts of 'the day it happened' would provide excellent material for the dramatic novelist. For example, one manager, after 15 years service, has a 10 minute 'interview' with a personnel officer who gives him 24 hours to leave with no reason given (images of espionage and deportation). Another manager received his sudden dismissal notice by personal delivery from his Director's secretary—7 o'clock in the morning at his home. A sales director had an enormous row with his boss over company policy; 1 week later a 'new man' had been brought in to replace him. A production manager returned from holiday to discover a 'reorganization'—no job. Several people talked of accusations of incompetence being made with no forewarning or prior discussion. Sales managers in highly competitive industries, such as computing, were often victims of their own sales figures—sometimes within 1 month of their joining the company. A number of participants described their utter dismay at attending what they thought was to be an interview for a promotion or salary rise, to be told that their services were no longer required. In all of these situations there was little feeling of gentlemanly conduct or concern—in radical contrast to the wooing and seduction that could characterize the recruitment and hiring process. It seems that an organization can spend considerable time and expense on hiring its professional personnel. In open competition the delights, challenges, and care accruing from company membership are openly advertised; the public relations machinery is well-oiled to do its smoothest best. In not-so-open competition an individual may be approached, flattered, and 'bribed' to join the company. Executive poaching is seen, by some, as very fair game. The individual who is offered a job can be made to feel really good; he is *wanted*. But when he is 'no longer required' the process seems markedly shorter and altogether more brutal. He is no longer a 'valued' person. Indeed his value was probably never more than his short-term economic and political ratings. When these fall, so does he. And he can find his own way out.

Redundancy left many deep scars. The feeling of being a pawn in remote and political games. The victim of rumour, half-truths, and uncertainty. Official expressions of company care, guaranteeing security, or a new job, would frequently evaporate when help was really needed. The tension and apathy that could grow up during a prolonged prelude to a redundancy decision could lead to a divisive climate—an attitude of 'If the company can do this to us we'll screw them for every penny they've got'. In practice, though, legal claims for compensation after redundancy usually stumbled over a number of possible technical hurdles, apart from the personal difficulties in pressing a claim while also trying to adjust to job loss.

Age and time unemployed. The different forms of impact are not easily explained by two other variables—age and time unemployed (Table B4). The average age is similar in each of the reaction categories. We do not, for example, find older people experiencing rejection, failure, or loss, more so than younger people. Likewise, the younger *and* older can view their job loss as a new opportunity and positive experience. Individual variations in impact appear to transcend age. So a man of 35 can feel the loss of 5 years personal effort in building up a business as much, if not more, than a man of 45 who has spent 5 years in a similar way. Their *relationship* to their work is critical here; not their age. Where age does seem more important is in getting back into work. This will be discussed in a later chapter.

One possible explanation of the variety of impact detected is that we are in fact picking up several different phases of impact according to the length of time an individual has been unemployed. Following this argument one might plausibly expect reject/failure and loss to be an early reaction, while acceptance and more positive reactions represent a form of adaptation over time. In fact the mean values for period unemployed are very similar in each of the impact categories (around 6–7 months), and they do not differ statistically. It seems that how long a person has been out of work, within the period represented in the study, does not reflect on the type of impacts we have observed.

Chapter 6

Threat

The logic of our analysis moves on from considering the impact of unemployment and its associated problems to the extent to which problems can become threatening. Those which threaten are potential stressors; those resulting in little or no threat unlikely to lead to stress.

The nature of threat

Threat is present when an important and valued aspect of one's life is under attack, or left vulnerable to attack, by unemployment. It was apparent from the interviews that such threat was frighteningly real to as many as 67 of the participants. The source of the threat could be in the circumstances surrounding the actual unemployment event, or in the consequences following the job loss.

Exactly what was threatened was far from uniform, reflecting the various forms of attachment that existed to the previous job, levels of anxiety, fears, family responsibilities, difficulty in the job market, and the motivational complexity and sensitivity of each person. Four general types of threat were apparent amongst these differences: *threat to pride and confidence, threat to competence and self-worth, threat to security*, and *threat to purpose and identity*. It was possible to associate one or more of these with each of the participants.

Pride and confidence

I feel deeply wounded—my integrity is knocked. What on earth can I say in interviews?

I'm so unsure of myself and I do so want to regain my confidence. If they say I can't teach my own subject, how can I ever get over that?

My pride has taken such a bashing—no one seemed to want to know me in the office when they knew I was going to be chucked out.

I need to control situations, but I'm fast losing my energy to work. I *need* challenging work. I'm constantly having to swallow my pride as things get worse.

I've asked for evidence of the complaint against me—but they say there's nothing in black and white. This has left me shattered and quite unprepared.

People say I've the ability to get on and work with other people, but I really don't see this in myself now.

Over recent months I've been feeling my confidence and capability knocked. What *am* I good for? Being self-employed all my life I've never gone on courses or anything. I'm not sure what I'm capable of doing for an employer.

I've had more and more reject letters—I'm constantly failing, which undermines my confidence. Everywhere I turn I am caught by my medical history.

These people were typically bemused and despairing. What they had taken for granted as intrinsic to their stature was there no more. For many work provided *the* source of their pride and confidence. The essential props had now been removed leaving them denuded and wounded.

Pride was frequently part and parcel of their *competence* and *self-worth* at work. This emerged as a related theme.

Competence and self-worth

Some psychologists (e.g. White, 1959) argue that the need to feel competent in dealing with one's world is one of the main human motivational forces. For a number of participants their job represented the main point of reference for their competence. At work they could exercise a range of abilities and see the results of their efforts. Formally and informally they could gain positive feedback on their levels of competence. The signs could be various: promotion; perks; salary rises; winning sales; increasing production and profit; praise from colleagues, superiors, and subordinate staff; personal feelings of 'things going right' because of one's own efforts or creativity; feeling 'stretched' at the end of the day for indefinable reasons; doing lots of things to one's full capacity. These features characterized their psychological work space. It was a capsule safe in its certainty and credibility, which provided them with the general message that they were competent human beings. Furthermore it was a very socially acceptable form of demonstrating competence. The job could legitimately fill most years of their life and appropriately help to sort out the less time-consuming roles, such as those of husband, wife, father, or mother.

But unemployment could bring a massive threat to all this. Typically the period up to the job loss could throw all the familiar signs into confusion, if not reversal. No longer was competence reinforced. No longer were there signs that one was a valued and worthy person, capable of performing a useful function. If a vestige of personal competence remained after the job loss it could have trouble surviving a few days, or at most a few weeks, without the familiar support of the job. Let us move closer to participants' own expressions of such difficulties:

So what's wrong with me? Maybe I have a personality problem. Do I pressurize people, unknown to me?

I've now failed a recent job *and* two before it. I put so much into preparing for the last job. What *am* I good at?

I always believed myself to be a 'people person', so to fail in a professional 'people' job has been very difficult for me. I was so committed to that view of life.

I chose the job—a grave error, an ego trip that failed. All the satisfaction that I wanted gradually failed to materialize. I've never had a break like this since I left school.

It was a new job. I was appointed to sort out their Parts Department. I was working 14–15 hours at the office and working at home—but I was having the satisfaction that I was getting things straight. Then I was asked to resign because I wasn't moving fast enough! I feel utterly disheartened.

I've been waking at night. What went wrong? How was I at fault? It grieves me terribly having to sign on. I must recover my status and self-respect.

I love work! People say I'm too concerned about work; I should get home and forget it. But where do they get their kicks—in the greenhouse?! My sense of achievement comes through my work. I've got to turn my energy back there.

It had taken me years to work up from the shop floor, and it was a really good job. Then I had this fearful argument with the Managing Director, and walked out. I really regret my action. All I've thrown up because of my impatience! What a defeat if I'm forced back to the shop floor!

I *failed* to provide the image and quantity required by the company. It's *my* responsibility, *my* failure. Being made redundant again really upsets me. The 6 months leading up to the redundancy was terrible—I had to shrink away and hide. I'm now reversing roles at home—my wife works. I find this a difficult situation to adjust to.

I just hate being out of work. I *really* feel in a rut. In no way do I want to watch Pinky and Perky on the television for the next 2 years. I believed it was a good idea to stay with one company rather than flit around. Look where this has left me!

I find it very difficult facing up to being made redundant because I *do* feel I'm a competent manager. I put so much into that organization. I really didn't want another job.

I've been made redundant twice before so I'm pretty cynical about company loyalty! When it happened, though, it knocked me right back on my heels. I felt remorseful that I had committed myself to that organization. My bad judgement. The added blow was to have to go cap in hand to the bank manager, something I've never done before.

Why me? What's wrong with me? I've lost the role for which I was trained. My fiancée wants me to take *any* job—but it's not that easy to move from being a professional to being a dustman.

I had to leave work to get married, but now I find myself thinking 'Who am I now?' Am I just a housewife important to my husband but to no-one else? Am I going to let my brain stagnate? I *need* to have challenge from work responsibility. I don't feel happy with just a domestic role. This feeling is overwhelming.

Self-doubt pervades these accounts. A few attempt to externalize the difficulties, but the shadow which eventually lingers is over *them*. Their job loss says something unpleasant about their competence—their decision-making ability, their interpersonal skills, their career choice, their proficiency in conducting their affairs. These threats are deep and painful.

Security

One thing a white collar job can provide is security. Security in the form of a regular income; a post which is a solid part of the organization, together with health, pension, and insurance rights. Staying loyal to the organization can further improve security as benefits can increase over time and through promotion. The company can cushion certain expenditures (a car, private education, and even holidays). It can also provide free, or inexpensive, sporting and other leisure facilities.

The secure image of the manager or professional is usually warmly received by the purveyors of credit in our society. So mortgage companies and banks are inclined to view members of such occupations as relatively secure risks on loans for houses, cars, boats, caravans, or other such accoutrements of life.

So the direct security rewards of the job can be considerable. Many managers and professionals would probably contend that they had a right to expect such security. They would have forgone a number of years of earning to gain specialized skills to bring to the organization. They would hold posts of considerable responsibility and authority, and they would work as many hours as necessary. In return for this, goes the argument, security should be high, if not guaranteed.

Some of the participants of the study found that loss of their security was *the* most disturbing thing to them. The edifice that they had erected around their jobs suddenly collapsed, penetrating all aspects of their life. Those who had received substantial financial compensation were, in practical terms, still secure. Emotionally, though, their insecurity could be acute. Although bills could be paid, the stream feeding the well had dried up. It was as if one was living on borrowed time:

Security has been the major thing. I'm worried for my wife—she's not sleeping properly with the insecurity. She has a similar experience with her parents so security is very important to her. We can survive until the end of the year, but what happens after that I don't know.

I do feel confused now. My unemployment was inevitable—it had to happen. But I don't want to repeat another failure. Roles are all confused at home; no one seems to know where they stand. Every month that passes increases our difficulties, especially the financial ones. I don't know where I am or where I belong.

I'm worried about my financial commitments—my property is a burden to me. There is the nagging feeling of having failed; of having to cut back after a failure. When you're in work you fantasize what you'd do if this would happen. Open a bed-and-breakfast? Go back to 9–5 on the shop floor? *Enjoy* life? But when the crunch comes you really begin to appreciate what you had.

We can't really manage financially—we've run out of resources now. We even get handouts of food parcels from our parents. The system *is* against me. All this produces some domestic strain.

My redundancy money is slipping away with nothing to show for it—this *really* worries me. I'm feeling I've wasted my life up to date and unless I do something now I'll never do anything.

I feel pretty badly about how this has come about. I have a large mortgage to meet plus other financial commitments. At 55 I haven't much time to experiment with new careers. I've been itching to apply my energy to something—but there's nothing. I really regret having stayed in the textile industry. My wife's not working and the redundancy pay wasn't that great.

I'm beginning to worry about money. I'm having stomach upsets, backaches, and headaches—things I've never had before. Inflation concerns me. My own area is difficult for employment—but where else can I go? I really miss my job.

Things have just started to become difficult financially. Now tension at home is increasing as my temper becomes more fragile. My wife nurses all day and gets home exhausted. Everything seems to be disintegrating.

I certainly don't feel I have an exciting capital sum. Just enough to keep me alive while I find another job. But where's my income now? I enjoyed my job thoroughly; it was challenging and exciting. But I'm disenchanted with large companies. I'm a single man and depend on my circle of friends—so I don't want to leave that.

These accounts draw our attention to some of the social and psychological ramifications of financial insecurity. Role relationships which functioned well when a regular income was taken for granted are now thrown into disarray. Indeed it becomes clear that much of the pattern of family life was the reciprocal of the participant's work role—something that was not considered when employed. The working wife is appreciated, but offers no real solution in the eyes of the male participants. Indeed, often she can only operate effectively if the husband can switch into her previous domestic role. This clearly is not easy when unemployment so fully occupies one's time and emotions.

The roots of insecurity are not necessarily just financial. The security which was threatened for some participants was that of a familiar, firm base in life. A protection against a variety of hostile forces, such as not knowing what to do, of time unfilled, of no clear way relating to family, friends, or oneself. Indeed, at this level, the fear of freedom of which Erich Fromm (1942) lucidly talks, is often implied:

I've been kicked out without a job! I now feel very lost. No job or supportive family. I urgently need the security of being part of a big organization.

Now I've spent a year in early retirement and I feel I need to retrieve some of the things I used to get at work—*to do something useful*. I've got a pension, so it's not the money. At home my wife constantly wants to know what I'm doing and where I'm going; the tension builds up. It's so much better that I have a job.

I enjoyed my work and success in the job. I feel redundancy was very unfair—it was an impersonal, uncaring organization. I really thought I'd found security. I now feel rejected, lonely, and wonder about my competence. Also I find my financial burdens overwhelming at the moment.

I didn't qualify for full redundancy pay, although my wife works, so that helps. But the job I take now *must* be secure. It's all getting mixed up with my marriage problems. It's quite worrying. I was effectively set adrift by my last boss—a rejection of me.

I personally feel I've had a miserable time in many ways. It really must have been my own wrong moves. I seem to have had a series of such problems in my career which makes it all very stressful. My mother is worried stiff and my father considers me a complete idiot. I now feel *very* insecure.

It has all been pretty traumatic. The worst has been my marriage break-up which has coincided with unemployment. A double emotional blow. I've felt very much alone over the past 10 months, especially without my wife's support. I've little confidence left.

Oh what I gave up. It was quite the wrong decision. It has left my wife and kids so vulnerable and it's *my* responsibility. I never realized that early retirement was effectively unemployment for me.

So I was edged out, but to what gain? Even now I know that nothing has changed in the company since I left. My cash won't last for ever and my wife can't work—she has a heart condition. I can't survive on my hobbies. So what *can* I do now?

I'm feeling lost—insecure. I've had lots of jobs, all involving self-employment with little reward. Basically I don't know what job I'd like. I keep failing, can't settle. I started a management course recently to get a new start, but failed the exams. I'm really frightened of getting wounded again.

The threat to security in unemployment underlines, in a particularly radical way, how much employment is needed by some to provide meaning in life. The perspective which is presented has a dimension not typically found in surveys of the employed. It is as if to know *un*employment is to know employment in a new light. Much of which was taken for granted at work, or of which one was unaware, becomes starkly evident after losing the job. It is analogous to suddenly appreciating the benefits of health when one is taken very sick for the first time.

Those who felt insecure in unemployment were often saying much more than 'I can't pay my bills'. The financial cushioning provided by regular employment was also a deeper psychological cushioning. The extent of this surprised even those who were not over-enamoured with their jobs and *thought* it would be pleasant to be unemployed.

Purpose and identity

The threat to security, competence, and self-worth was sometimes expressed quite fundamentally in terms of *raison d'être*. It shook some people's very belief in themselves; their sense of purpose and identity were thrown into confusion.

I find a lot of personal internal turmoil which wasn't there before my unemployment. In a way the unemployment has set off questioning everything. The most shattering thing for me is questioning what I thought was a solid belief in religion. I feel I'm getting more and more remote from my belief. I now realize I was far more involved in my job than I ever thought. Maybe this covered up these problems.

The job was my life. It also provided me with everything I value—particularly my personal freedom.

With a job I could get married and have a house and kids. What's all my education for if I chuck it away on a low-paid manual job?

No-one really wants to know you when you're on the 'outside'. Employers are very wary of me. All this has really knocked me for six—it takes a while to stand on your feet again.

The unemployment has sparked my need for some *life purpose*. I must structure my life accordingly, but to what? I need to be *involved*. I have a strong sense of purpose for *something*. But am I thinking straight, or am I fooling myself? It's a make-or-break decision which makes me feel very anxious.

I'm in a position of limbo. I feel confused and uncertain. I don't know where I am or where I'm going, or whether I should direct my career in a different field. My own professional group wants me back, but I just don't know.

The right job is so important because it's all I've got. I'm anxious about occupying myself and not to be the 'retired' employee who disintegrates.

I really feel so lost without a *regular* daily activity. It's all bits and pieces now. My work provided a long, absorbing day. I now lack a focal point in life. How long can I stand this?

We are again reminded that employment can act as a psychic glue; it holds an individual together in aim, purpose, and identity. Without employment those activities, routines, and relationships which characterize daily effort are missing. An individual has no clear reference points against which he can identify himself and his competence. The psychological integration that employment can provide draws upon the rewards of personal contacts at work—colleagues and friends, the familiar understood tasks and processes, the sense of history, security, and belonging, and the mutual reflection of these in domestic and social roles. They can take some time to mature and stabilize—to eventually become 'internalized' as an unquestioned sense of being. Indeed a person can *become* his job—his occupational identity and other self-images becoming inextricably fused. Job loss can harshly overturn this, leaving the individual feeling vulnerable and wary.

Low threat

One-third of the participants were quite unlike those we have just described. There was little that was threatening for them in their unemployment. Their statements suggested two rather different reasons behind this. The first was founded in their relationship to their previous job. The job was entrapping, stressful, monotonous, or stultifying, consequently job loss, for *whatever* particular reason, was a positive release. Far from attacking their competence, integrity, confidence, worth, and sense of creativity, it opened opportunities to *achieve* these unfulfilled needs. Sixteen people expressed their position in these terms. They described job loss *reactively*. What they felt now was in direct contrast to what they experienced in the job, and it was these comparisons which dominated their thoughts and expressions—'This is how lousy things were at work, now life feels good and hopeful' was the typical sentiment.

But there was a remarkably clear split between these individuals and 12 others who did not talk in such contrasts. They also expressed their job loss as positive opportunity, but in a *proactive* form. It was not their previous job experiences which made them feel particularly good now. It was more simply that they were the sort of people who were characteristically forward-looking. They were optimistic, philosophical, flexible, and creative when faced with a problem. Thus, fairly pervasive and adaptive personality characteristics would 'see them through'.

This is not to suggest that the reactive individuals were lacking in such adaptive fortitude. Some were clearly a subtle mix of reactive and adaptive characteristics. Furthermore, within the interviews many proactive participants would reveal that their jobs had been unrewarding in many ways. It was more a matter of what each person took as the appropriate starting point for personal adaptation. There were those who would focus on the past to make sense of the present and future, and there were those who were unconcerned with (or who blanked off) the past. For the latter the 'here and now' was what was important. One suspects that they would handle most life changes in a similar manner.

Let us look at some illustrative quotations:

Reactive low threat

I felt trapped in the job. I was terrified by my boss—she would intimidate me. For ages I didn't know what to do because it was so important for me to be successful. Then suddenly I came to terms with it and gave in my notice.

I was in this dead-end job for $1\frac{1}{2}$ years. It was awful. There was nightwork which put stress on the family. I love my family but had no time to talk to them. I was very unhappy, but not now.

It's a relief to leave. The job caused me enormous stress—broken promises and shabby treatment all along.

I was working too hard. It ruined communications with my family. I can now start again.

The redundancy came as a heaven-sent opportunity to get out—a clear crossroads in my life. I feel like someone who has been released from 20 years in prison. I've felt euphoric—I'm free!

I've had three reactions. Firstly, thank goodness for that. I don't have to worry about the figures again. Secondly, I've always wanted to change my professional line. And thirdly, now's the opportunity for that long holiday we've always promised ourselves.

The job was full of unreasonable pressures. So after I left I thought 'Thank God, I'm a happy man!' I'm now able to take stock of myself and re-appraise. I'm now more hopeful than I've been for a long time.

After leaving I felt relief in some way. The job was so monotonous and predictable. I felt pangs of regret leaving old mates, but that's all. I lose no sleep over it. I'm now eagerly planning my own business.

I find this period very cleansing, away from the synthetic world of inter-national trade. I miss all my friends, but apart from that there are no regrets. I now need to form a new life, find a new challenge.

I'm getting sick of my work as a consultant, living off false pretences. So many of my reports are bullshit—perhaps 1 per cent of my work is tangible and useful. You *can't* do it purely for the money—I'm getting tired of the fat and famine of it. I now need to make some career decision—something I can do without getting uptight about it.

I left teaching to take a catering course, but I wasn't fast enough or skilled enough to keep up. I became very edgy and unhappy. So I resigned and immediately felt happier and relaxed. I'm now taking things in my stride before striking out again.

A great sense of relief at not doing a job I didn't like. I must now seek the right career.

For 10 years I feel I've been shut in by my job—a bit like a pit pony. Since I've been away from there I can see there's a whole new world.

I felt so unhappy in my job—couldn't wait to get out. I was praying for redundancy. Orders were dropping dramatically and a hatchet man was appointed. It was great when I left. I'm convinced that what happened to me was a good thing.

I had to resign because of continuing ill health. I now realize that I was trapped in that teaching job—I didn't know how fast time was passing. Now my health is better I want to go back to my earlier career as a practising scientist.

Leaving my job abroad was a great relief—something off my shoulders. I didn't *feel* unemployed when it happened. I now feel released and relaxed looking forward to a new life.

I'm not regretting I've left—and I don't think I ever will. Before redundancy I was *so* lethargic—couldn't do anything after work. Now this feeling has gone completely!

What these people are reacting to varies in emphasis, but the core issue appears to be feeling trapped in an unfulfilling job. The image of time spent, day in and day out, enmeshed in activities which have little or no intrinsic reward—a picture more reminiscent of some blue collar jobs. Feelings of excitement in the job, being stretched and challenged, were unknown—or at best a faded memory. Some would vividly recount how their jobs had encroached into their home life, damaging family relations.

Proactive low threat

I'm a perpetual optimist. I believe that as one door closes another opens. I just don't worry.

I see this as a new beginning. I'm looking for new opportunities.

It's a real challenge looking for a job. One, perhaps, I'd prefer not to have—but having got it I'm not too dissatisfied with it.

I've made the break, and that's that. I'm not one to sit on my backside all day. I daresay it doesn't take much readjusting. I don't publicize being out of work, but I *feel* released from a trap.

It's a bit like a long holiday which I *know* can't last. I'm not over-worried though—there are plenty of choices open to me.

I need to exploit the advantages of my unemployment. I feel adaptable. I like change and variety so I am optimistic.

I now take unemployment as an *opportunity* for me to reassess my direction and life. I've fought against simply accepting the situation.

I've looked to the future and I'm not depressed. I'm not too bitter about my dismissal—I was offered good compensation.

Doing odd jobs, like driving a tractor, for the past 2 years unemployment has been great mental therapy for me. Now I'm keen and confident to get back to industry. I'll enjoy the rest of my life.

I thought I'd been let down a bit—they said they'd look after me but these were false promises. I feel optimistic and philosophical about things. I guess I'm pretty armoured against stress, I've had one or two heavy knocks in my life already.

I'll always survive, even if I hit the bottom. I'm happier now than any time in the last 10 years. I feel it will come together—hope I'm not overconfident.

These accounts ring of uncomplicated optimism. A simple statement of 'This is where I am, so there's no point in crying over spilt milk.' They are not interested in their past because it is irrelevant to their current feelings, or to their future.

Three participants clearly expressed both reactive and proactive responses. Their jobs were very unsatisfactory and it did influence how they felt. Yet this was tempered by a strong streak of optimisim.

> I've no financial worries. I've got a year's redundancy pay plus extras. Also my wife is in a well-paid, secure job. So I confidently look to the future. Actually it sounds a bit silly, but I'm not sorry I lost the job. I was a damn good export manager, but I didn't really enjoy it. I'd rather be painting gutters! But this is the first time I've had a chance to view it that way.

> I try to look for a silver lining. Being at home, having the time to reflect and think. I've really wondered whether I've been a bloody fool to work like this all these years. What has it done for me and my family?

> Although I enjoyed the work it wasn't really my line. I'm very disappointed, but there's no point in being bitter or unhappy. I've now got to get on with finding something new.

Threat and impact

Impact may be seen as the meaning of the initial contact with unemployment, and threat one of the consequences of that contact. But the form of contact, and type of consequences, are very closely related. Of those experiencing threat, 90 per cent talked of the impact in terms of rejection, failure, or loss. Eighty per cent of those finding the impact an acceptable or positive experience were not threatened by the job loss. So impact and threat are similarly coloured for most participants, and one could see both processes intermixed within individuals' expressions and perceptions.

Theoretically, one would expect impact to precede threat, as outlined in the model of stress in unemployment. But sorting out just when the threat emerges is difficult, if not impossible, from retrospective accounts. Indeed, both processes could be so closely related in time, and hence interrelated psychologically, that it could be an unproductive and perhaps rather silly venture to attempt to do so. So, for example, the impact of shock, failure, and rejection could speedily and imperceptibly merge into feelings of threat to competence and esteem. Thereafter both are mixed up in one's awareness and concern.

It is noteworthy that impact and threat are similarly toned, but they are not similarly constructed, as our analysis has shown. Each has its own dimensional constituents and its own subtleties. Furthermore the emotional reactions do not match perfectly. Five participants who had strong feelings of regret and disillusionment on losing their jobs did not show evidence of feeling threatened. Conversely, eight people who described their initial reaction to unemployment in very positive terms, went on to express a range of different feelings of threat.

Chapter 7

Coping and Stress

The experience of threat is the prelude to stress. How successful a person is at coping with threat determines his level of stress. Coping, as discussed in Chapter 2, may take the form of inactivity, avoidance, or confrontation—the former two being direct defences against anxiety. Mastering the threat is the ultimate form of coping with stress—a result possible from confrontation, but unlikely from inactivity or avoidance.

The tape-recordings and transcripts of all participants who were experiencing threat were examined to see how they were coping. Evidence was sought on what they were actually doing about their predicament. What tactics or forms of reported behaviour characterized their coping?

Two groups emerged. The smaller group, 12 people, were showing signs of coping with their threat. The majority, of 55 people, were failing to cope. Let us first look at the way the different forms of coping relate to measured stress, strain, and self-esteem. Our framework on stress in unemployment suggests:

1. those who are successfully mastering the threat from unemployment should experience little stress or strain compared with those who are failing to do so;
2. those experiencing no threat should feel little or no stress or strain;
3. coping with threat, or experiencing no threat, should leave participants feeling more positive about themselves.

The trends of the relevant scores (see Appendix C) support all of these expectations. It would seem that coping with threat can be critical in determining psychological and physical well-being during unemployment. But what exactly is the nature of such coping, and failure to cope? The qualitative data provide us with some clues.

Successfully coping with threat

The 12 individuals who had managed to cope with the threat from unemploy-

62

ment did so mainly through two different routes, each indicating different facets of confrontation. The first route was *direct action* of some sort:

> At this very moment my morale is considerably boosted. My efforts to find a job, after 1½ years, suddenly look hopeful. I have two jobs in the pot, both fitting what I want. One even *asked* for someone who was in their early 50s because they have 'polish' by that time! You've no idea how good this sounded because I was getting a real hang-up about my age.

> I've gone through the Army resettlement process, and I'm applying for jobs. It's very strange dealing with the interviews, but I'm still learning, supported by the Army.

> The household chores irritate me and I really dread ending up enclosed within four walls. So I'm not letting my job fade away. I've applied for teaching posts and I'll keep at it.

> I'm doing some private language teaching and I write articles. I've set myself a 3 month target to find a *different* business to work in. Otherwise I'll consider the travel business again, or further studying.

> Up to recently my failure to get a job has undermined my confidence. I received more and more reject letters, and I was desperately applying for anything and everything. I kept reducing my aspirations as my medical history was constantly used against me. But now two good things have happened. Firstly, I'm getting married. And secondly PER have been really helpful to me. I can see something emerging.

In these cases each person has taken some specific action in the job market. None has actually got a job, but they are confident and hopeful in their expectations. This *anticipatory* success in removing the threat and retrieving their pride, confidence, competence, or security, is sufficient to reduce the potency of the threat and avoid stress, at least for the time being.

The second confrontation approach was based on *reconstruing* the situation in a way which laid the foundation for direct action. The confrontation was symbolic. It was a way of personally coming to terms with the fears and anxieties associated with the threat by carefully examining oneself and one's predicament, and then harnessing energy to find a replacement for the lost job:

> I've been thinking and thinking about this situation and I now think I've worked through these fears. I *accept* that I'll not retrieve my previous career. I can now turn my energies outwards rather than inwards. My wife is now much more understanding and sympathetic, which really helps.

> I'm now prepared to go *anywhere* so long as I get retrained. During the last few years I've only applied for local jobs, but now that's got to change—I'll go further afield. I'll also try for further study.

I've had to take charge of life before, like when I lost my mother. So I *can* do it! I'd like someone to lean on, but now I'm separated from my husband, there is no-one. So that's that.

I've recently seen a friend who was made redundant—he was completely shattered. From that moment I was determined never to react like that, and I haven't. I now see this as a temporary set-back. I'll just have to climb the ladder again.

OK, I'm confused and uncertain, but I *know* this and I'm handling it. My professional training helps me. I can manage my anxieties.

I guess I don't really feel the urgency of it yet. I haven't sat around un-employed—I've tried to get myself moving. But I'm not going to be forced by husband or family into getting the first job that comes along.

One person had adapted more defensively. Having failed to secure a job he adopted an avoidance strategy by immersing himself in attractive alternative pursuits.

I just can't seem to get anywhere with the firms I've applied to. But I've thrown myself into work with my family, land, and animals. This is satisfying and relaxing—but can it last forever?

Failing to cope with threat

The majority of those who had failed to cope with threat had taken some direct action to improve their situation, but had not succeeded. Their high stress was, in terms of our framework, a compound of anxiety from the still-present threat *and* the personal burden of further failure.

Forty participants talked of their attempts to obtain a job. Many were methodical, flexible, and exceedingly energetic in confronting their task. In stress terms they had sized up the threat and tackled it head-on. But their considerable efforts had been in vain. For example:

I was determined to get another job straight away, but I didn't. I've chased up all my contacts and used the newspapers—tried everything. But no job offers despite 12–14 interviews. Even downgraded jobs are closed to me, although I don't really want to downgrade. Employers are suspicious—why, with my experience, was I applying for a job beneath me? My wife is pushing me to downgrade—I conflict with her on this. It's wrong to downgrade.

I've been looking for a job for 4 months. I've always got replies and interviews. In one I reached the fourth interview only to find that the job didn't fit me at all! You can imagine how flat I felt! I was very bitter. I'm on 10 or 11 agency books and I'm still on the short-list of the first job I applied for! At first my lack of success didn't bother me. But then I became so low. I now get tummy upsets, vomiting, and I need Valium to get to sleep.

All the contacts came to nothing. Direct approaches to companies have come to very little—few respond. Virtually no progress in the last 4 months—I'm approaching a dead end. Maybe the word is getting round that I'm contacting lots of people—'what's wrong with this guy!'

I've really struggled over the past 12 months. Reduced targets, salary bands, travelled all over the country. As yet I haven't had a single job offer. I've been called for interviews and been shortlisted. I've made 80 applications and had around 50 interviews. Even a further education grant has been refused despite top references. All this has hit me particularly hard.

I've applied for 17–18 jobs and had seven or eight interviews. Now I'm really feeling depressed. One perfect-sounding job this morning in *no way* lived up to its description. I had an interview last week and was told I'd hear straight away—but nothing. This morning I dented the car—I wasn't able to concentrate properly.

I thought that I'd soon get another job, but how wrong I was! I soon got interviews with other companies, but I was always rejected. Probably all of them would have got in touch with my ex-boss who would have given me a very bad reference. I've been rejected by so much of my own professional market that I've even tried for car salesman jobs—and I haven't even got those! So I'm now barred from work even in the area in which I've most experience

Since my unemployment there have been no positions advertised in my trade. I have made 35 direct contacts, but nothing. It brings you down a bit when you don't get interviews. Each time I get an application form I get all expectant. I always research the company—such a waste of time. So all this has made me very low. My age, 53, always seems against me.

In the first week or two I tried everything to recover my status and self-respect. I wrote letters off to everyone I knew. At least one letter a day for application forms and enquiries. But nothing came of it. I just don't get replies or acknowledgements. Often companies promise to contact or give information, but nothing comes. That *really* disappoints me. People shouldn't be able to just walk over you.

I've achieved 60 per cent interviews from 60–70 applications. My morale has been boosted at the interview stage, only then to be told that there were more suitable candidates. It's hit me recently when I received three refusals without anything around the corner. It's hurt me more in the personal approaches I've made to ex-colleagues without any response. Or rejection out of hand after checking with my previous employer, with no opportunity to counter previous employers' judgements. Sometimes I've been very demoralized at being rejected as not suitable without being able to find out why. They say 'others were more suitable', then I see the job readvertised! I cannot get the truth and honesty from them that they expect of me.

The desperation at the constant frustration of 'getting nowhere' strongly pervaded many of the accounts:

I just can't get a position—constant rejection. I've filled in so many forms to get just one interview which didn't come to anything. The results are always negative. I can't understand it—it's awful.

I've made over 50 applications with no success. They say I'm too old at 54. I've registered with all the employment bureaux, but nothing. *Is* it my age? Or is it because I'm from East Africa? I'm now feeling very depressed sitting at home doing nothing. I've worked all my life, and I'm not being given a chance. On some forms I even say I'll give 2 weeks without pay to show my abilities—but still no replies!

I have 20 applications in process, but I've had only two interviews, and I can see I'm approaching a panic situation. I *must* know where I am before then. Also, should I accept a post in my previous trade which I *know* is shrinking? I *know* I shouldn't, but maybe I'll be forced to.

Overall I've made 200–250 applications to schools. Not all reply. I've had around six interviews. Maybe I've been *too* honest on my application forms —but I'm an honest man. I've had between 30 and 40 jobs in my career, of which I'm not proud. I've had nervous/chest problems which has kept me off work for long periods. To an interviewer looking at my CV it looks bad. Also, over 40 and diabetes and up go the shutters. I'm now a temporary supply teacher but the work isn't coming in. I'll teach *anything*. The demoralized feeling I have is just out of this world.

I've done a lot of ringing up or writing. I'm being told that either I am too old, or asked why do I want a lower-level job. You can't convince them that you *want* to step 'down'. But I don't *want* to aim higher!

I've been trying consultancy, but business is darned intermittent. The last assignment ended 11 months ago. I'm now really back where I was 10 years ago, but several thousand pounds worse off and 10 years older. I've made 150 cold calls, applied for 64 jobs, written for overseas posts, had 12 interviews and been offered one job selling life insurance. I didn't want that. Consultancy is such an oversubscribed profession—some offer ridiculously low rates just to keep their hand in. So all this has been bloody hell for me—doctor says I'm an anxious type.

I've had one job for 2 months, but they didn't like my medical record—my nervous breakdown—so they asked me to leave. I've had 15 or 16 interviews in the last 4 months, six second interviews and one third interview. But it's a buyers' market. They can lead you up the garden path until the last moment. They can tell several people they're 'number one' on the list. I've been promised decisions—but nothing comes. This lackadaisical approach starts to erode one's confidence in people—it hits you hard.

We get an overall picture of people who are turning their skills towards their own problems, but with little success. Constantly unrewarded effort leaves them more and more dispirited and confused. Hopes are raised when an interview is granted, or when reaching a short list—only to be dashed with a refusal letter. Or, perhaps even worse, to hear nothing at all. From this grows the feeling of being used and exploited in a 'buyers' market'—a mere pawn amongst other pawns.

Some noted how fast their circle of colleagues and contacts disintegrated, leaving them feeling even more *persona non grata*. Others noted the acute dilemma of finding that the only saleable skills that they had were those specific to the dying industry from which they had just come. Retraining was nice in theory, but in practice it required a motivation and ability to learn, or relearn. Not all participants could neatly step into this mould, nor were appropriate training facilities and finance always available.

Certain participants were disabled rather more quickly in their job hunt. Their failures were, psychologically speaking, no less stressful than the others; however, their sensitivity to rejection was greater:

I asked to re-take the test I'd failed, but it's not allowed. Now at 59 it's been very difficult to get a job. One interview I got was terminated when they learned my age. Others don't even reply to me. I'm going round in circles between different agencies. I couldn't even get a commissionaire's job, right at the bottom of the ladder! I'm in a really ambiguous situation now, not knowing what to do.

I had a crack at consulting, but with no success. I reapproached my old firm, but was rejected. I feel so depressed—sitting at home getting more and more despondent.

Prior unemployment, or a chequered job history, added to some people's difficulties:

I feel depressed. I have 3–4 applications in process and I've a couple of accountancy interviews. But my last two jobs are of no help to me; I have difficulty talking about them in job interviews. In your 20's all this can't be so bad. By 41 your sense of humour becomes strained. It's not like a TV comedy show where the comedian can mess up every job and laugh it off. My wife has been trying to get me to change my line for years—I'm really too stubborn and proud. It's like banging your head against a brick wall. The future must take over.

My dismissal keeps arising as a problem, and I haven't found a job I want yet. I'd now like a business of my own to regain my security and also some of the smallest comforts I've been without in the last 3 years. I've really suffered privations.

I've had around six interviews, but I know I don't interview well. I've been brought up to *underrate* my abilities. I seem to be mistrusted by interviewers who see I have had many short-term jobs. They think I'll leave them.

Rarely were the problems of finding a job neatly separated from other life demands. The energy required to maintain direct action was frequently considerable, so concurrent (or consequent) difficulties in other spheres of one's life could soon take their toll. Marriage problems were amongst these:

I've kept information on jobs so I've used this to write off for vacancies. But many of the jobs that would suit me require freedom to travel around, and nights away from home. How can I do that? It would be very stressful for my wife. At the same time it's really urgent to sort out my marriage problems. I can't share my job problems with my wife.

I'm writing letters and filling in applications and I'm really hopeful that I'll get the job I want. But my marriage has been severely strained which confuses the job problem. She wants a separation, which is a very bad time for me when I'm unemployed.

For others it was different facets of the role relationship with the spouse:

I just can't see the wood for the trees. I've become jealous of my wife's better education. I have awful problems with tests—keep failing them. I've been applying for jobs like my previous one but they've turned out to be below me or well above me.

My age, 57, is a bit difficult. I've written in reply to 150 advertisements and to 50 local companies. I've also used the old-boy network. I've reached a couple of short lists but nothing concrete has emerged. So 3 months without success. Maybe I need to start my own business. I can take the change of status, but can my wife leave the 'senior executive' circle? Also, what about a pension?

Confrontation and avoidance

The reactions that have been described represent the feelings following failure at direct action. But some had moved from such failure to try to find ways of preventing further escalation of their stress. For example, they would nervously flirt with a few job applications without any strong commitment to pursuing them; they would engage in less threatening distractions such as hobbies or pastimes, or they would simply do nothing. This self-protective disengagement from the job hunt is illustrated in the following accounts:

I've sought travel jobs because that's what I'm best at. I've had one interview and I suspect my last employer put in a bad word for me. I'm not sure how I'll get over this. I have immersed myself in hobbies to stop me going quietly mad, but this only partly helps.

I've had four interviews to date and three refusals. Generally I've plenty of job ideas—it's *getting up* and *carrying them out* which is the problem. I don't really talk about my emotions.

In three years I've managed to make only six applications and had two interviews. But people don't respond—I've been let down. Now I'm really in a limbo state. I seem to box myself in. I can't find a solution. I've achieved nothing. I'm becoming so irritable, sick and isolated.

I *keep* meaning to apply for jobs outside of my field of sales management, but I just don't do it! I've sent out a few applications for sales management jobs, and I actually got shortlisted for one. But I was relieved when I didn't get it! I'm so unsure of where I should be.

I've written lots of letters, but with very little positive response. I've refused two interviews because it was underselling myself. I *mustn't* drop salary or I'll be lost for the future; my whole lifestyle and status is at stake. I now can't do anything because I feel so hurt.

I've had one recent job interview, but that's all. I really don't know which way to turn—I feel overwhelmed by everything.

I did freelance work which took my mind off things, but it didn't get me any nearer to something I *really* wanted to do. I've applied for a few jobs but didn't do too well. The promises of assignments just collapsed.

Nowadays every time I get an application form it takes longer to fill in. They lie on my desk for weeks. What's the use! Maybe I can't express myself at interviews, but I was fresh with enthusiasm at the beginning. The waiting is awful—3, 4, 5 weeks until a decision. I don't feel happy. The longer it drags on the less optimistic I feel.

I've been applying for jobs and lazing about. I've been for four selling jobs, but I'm a bit edgy in interviews—not used to them! I'm quite nervous about my capabilities. This surprised me after all the difficulties I coped with in my own company. I realize that I sometimes threaten the manager who is interviewing me—I look too qualified in some ways!

I'm now being so ultra-cautious it's ridiculous. I've operated a switch-off mechanism. Despite all the demands I just stop—do nothing.

These individuals have, in effect, begun to withdraw from the front line of the battle. But their retreat has simply underlined the hopelessness of the situation to them. While they are no longer experiencing further direct failures or humiliation, their basic inability to cope with their threat is already established, as is their high level of stress.

Ineffective defence

There were 15 participants whose attempts to defensively cope with the anxiety from unemployment dominated their adaptation. They were in such emotional confusion that they were in no position to confront their problem conceptually, or in direct action terms. Yet they indicated, in various ways, that their defences were not fully protecting them. Their awareness of the threat was very apparent, as were their strenuous efforts to keep it at bay. The forms of defence were very much of the avoidance/inaction type. At its extreme, attempting to escape completely from any contact with the problem:

I don't know what to do now—I just want to hide away in a corner.

The problem is unsolved—I'm confused and worried. I'm still searching myself for an answer, but can't find one.

Sometimes I feel I'll never get a job—I do lack confidence in myself. I seem to get tied up in getting my house in order. I realize I should have started looking for a job earlier, but I just don't know which direction to take.

I daydream of being in a reasonable job without working all hours of the day. But with all my past mishaps I'm a bit frightened to go after jobs.

I've registered with PER and a few agencies—but I haven't managed to do much else. I've no heart for it, or anything.

I feel a bit trapped. I can't clarify what will happen to my pension if I get a job—so I haven't done anything yet. I've thought about things I really like doing—but maybe these are pipe dreams. It will all catch up with me by the end of the year—I *am* worried.

I'm so confused. I've looked at various jobs but I haven't a clue which direction to take.

I'm perplexed and unsure about what I may do. Money's getting tight and I'm feeling I need to do something. But what?

My loss of religious faith is difficult to cope with. It's stunned me that unemployment should have done this to me. I'm in such personal turmoil.

As a kid I learned to blot things out when I was very anxious—a protective mechanism. And this is what I've been doing. I've become inactive, but the cold problem keeps re-emerging. I'm scared of committing myself to anything.

I've done virtually nothing about finding a job. I don't talk about my problems with others. I'd have financial problems if my wife didn't work. Perhaps we'll emigrate—get out of this country, which is going down the tube anyway.

I didn't do a thing for 6 weeks because PER were helping. But nothing happened. Then I started making searches myself, but struggling with myself during this time. My feelings of remorse and depression have only slightly lightened. I really have to get up and *do* something.

Some of these people projected a feeling of heavy inertia, of being overwhelmed with their difficulties and *knowing* they were overwhelmed. A job was somewhere, distantly, outside of the quicksands that were engulfing them. Keeping a semblance of 'togetherness' was a considerable achievement in itself.

The primacy of the job

Reflecting upon the efforts, and anguish, expressed by participants it is noteworthy that, with just one exception, everybody saw getting a job as the end-point of their endeavours.

While this observation may not appear particularly profound, the *unquestioned* assumption that 'working for a living' as *the* way of living does seem to have important implications for the way we organize ourselves. Even those people who described their past employment as a shackle to their freedom and health sought a *better* job as a solution—not some alternative way of satisfying their needs. The necessity to earn money is one obvious reason for this. Formal employment provides for this—but sometimes little more. However this is not a sufficient reason because there were a number of participants who through stage of career, personal wealth, or large redundancy payment, claimed sufficient finance to last them the rest of their lives. It does seem that the social and psychological safety net of 'the job' is very deeply ingrained in our cultural subconsciousness. Any 'employment' outside of some formal job will not easily form a *central* life endeavour. Hobbies, leisure pursuits and other personal interests exist relative to the job. Indeed to engage too much of one's time in these activities can invite social castigation—implications of 'being on holiday' or not taking one's responsibilities seriously. Irregular employment, switching jobs or careers, or working at 'fringe' activities (communes, self-help organizations) can bring similar strictures. Despite the growing level of white collar unemployment, a frequent concern amongst the participants was the stigma attached to their unemployed status—a theme to be developed in Chapter 11.

The one person who did not fit this pattern is worthy of further mention. He was a young mathematics graduate who had achieved his own, unusual, modus operandi:

> After $2\frac{1}{2}$ years unemployed I've got used to it. The carrot of employment is no longer attractive—a bit mouldy around the edges. Unemployment is a way of life to me—I'm cynical about the job market. Whatever job I get now must be considered against the benefits of unemployment—personal freedom, independence and no fixed hours of work. I miss the money, but I get by.

This man wished to give the impression that much personal satisfaction could be achieved outside of the context of work. His constant lack of success in the job market effectively *forced* him to consider the possibility of a life of unemployment. He discovered that there were other ways of 'happily' organizing his time and these had now become as much a part of his taken-for-granted world as being in a job. What is perhaps particularly interesting is that some of the words he uses to describe the benefits of unemployment ('freedom', 'independence') are exactly those that other participants used to describe the rewards of employment.

These observations have coalesced as I write this chapter and as I digest the implications of participants' comments. During my counselling they nagged me, but in a less coherent way. When someone did not know 'what to do with his life' I found myself automatically running through different occupational niches which might fit in with his personality and circumstances. This seemed to be welcomed by the participant and it was, I suppose, something I could readily do. But it also illustrated to me that *my* alternatives were no less hide-bound than theirs. I could offer no magical creative leap—no viable alternatives. Indeed, I was, perhaps, at my most radical when I would counsel a delay before re-entering the job market, explore whether or not the trappings of a career were *needed*, and discuss whether leisure interests could provide a key to new life activities. The typical response was one of attentive anxiety. In one way or another they would tell me that (a) a delay could accentuate feelings of being an 'incomplete person', aggravating their stigma, (b) their lives were far too attuned to the job/career syndrome to opt out at this stage (or any stage?), and (c) leisure interests are not really the stuff from which real jobs are made.

A related issue was that I could sometimes see little that was intrinsically satisfying or challenging for a participant in the job to which he was turning. But I would feel myself very much seduced by his feelings of financial and emotional security. These appeared as overriding issues for him, especially if he felt rejected and threatened. *Any* job seemed better than none, to restore some sense of normality to life—or was it? Was I colluding with him in an 'unhelpful' way? What was I counselling him towards in the longer term? Back to a 'lousy' job? What sort of 'patch-up' was I doing?

These thoughts left me with mixed emotions—part of me feeling helpful and the other part feeling impotent. It seemed I was caught in a process of 'live now and maybe pay later'. It starkly illustrated the limitation of *individual* help in unemployment where the roots of the difficulties can lie in more social, structural, and political forces. Yet if a man is starving from lack of work you do not read him a text on the evils of capitalism. We shall return to these points anon.

Chapter 8

Six Months On

A follow-up questionnaire was sent to all participants 6 months after their attendance on the programme. The response was 72 per cent, after reminders. The time taken to return the questionnaire varied from 6 months to 12 months, the average time being 8 months.

There were three major sub-groups amongst the total of respondents: those who were *still unemployed* (19 people), those who had *found a job that satisfied them* (37 people), and those who were *in employment but were unhappy about their position* (16 people). Qualitative data on reported feelings, behaviour, and problems were available for all 72 respondents. However, the structured instruments were completed by rather fewer—57 in all. Seventeen of these were still unemployed, 28 satisfactorily employed, and 12 unsatisfactorily employed.

Stress, strain, and self-esteem—a general picture

A general, overall image of the participants at follow-up is available from the patterns of response to the stress, strain, and self-esteem questionnaires. We can look at (a) how they appear absolutely in the three major sub-groups, and (b) specific changes over the 6-month period. The detailed statistics are presented in Tables D1 to D7 in Appendix D.

Summarizing, it is noteworthy that despite small numbers involved the trends were sometimes sufficiently powerful to indicate certain unexpected differences. Most prominent amongst these was the high level of stress and strain and low self-esteem of those 12 people who felt unsuited to their jobs. They were experiencing *more* difficulties than those still unemployed and showed signs of more strain and lower self-esteem than 6 months before. It seems that unfulfilled expectations after re-employment may serve to exacerbate threat and reinforce feelings of failure. In a naive sense the ultimate solution to unemployment has been found—a new job. But if that job turns out to meet few of a participant's threatened needs then his actions at coping have been singularly unsuccessful. This point will be further explored shortly with the qualitative data. The very opposite pertains to those who have found a job which suits them. The effects for them appear markedly beneficial: stress drops to a negligible level and self-esteem improves.

Adding a further 6 months to unemployment does not seem to change things for those 17 participants still without a job. Although they had now been job-less for an average of 15 months, their levels of stress, strain, and self-esteem were very much as they were 6 months previously. There is certainly no evidence, on these measures, of an overall worsening of reported psychological and physical reactions as these people move into longer-term unemployment.

Let us now move into the subtleties and idiosyncrasies of adaptation and reaction by examining the qualitative reports.

Follow-up—qualitative data

Some participants wrote lengthily and thoughtfully about their circumstances; others were briefer in their words. All of the responses were read, and re-read, prior to summarizing and classifying. As before, the sorting of the statements was guided by the model of stress; thus the perception of problems in relationship to initial threat and coping became a key feature of the analysis. But also, as before, the expression and meaning of these phenomena is most adequately revealed through participants' actual words.

Still unemployed

Nineteen people were without jobs. Twelve of these were still failing to cope with the consequences of their job loss, their stress and despair becoming progressively more entrenched:

> I felt ready to move ahead after the course but now I'm deflated and depressed. I've applied for 80 positions unsuccessfully. Women over 45 are no competition for younger females who can take lower salaries. I'm told there are 800 unemployed teachers in my county. I could paper the walls with my unsuccessful applications. I'm now resigned to never work permanently again and realize that if someone has to fail in life it might as well be me as I have no family or close friends.

> As I heard nothing from PER I eventually signed off. It was a waste of time. I really *need* to get down to serious job hunting and I'm considering moving, but I can't seem able to. I'm despondent because it's not an easy thing to do at my age. It's not the best experience to live from day to day. It really has a bad effect on friends and relations. During unemployment the contrasts in success become so noticeable—I'm *so* aware of friends and relations who have 'made it'.

I'm still unemployed but I've attended two courses. I've written in reply to many advertisements and made some direct approaches to companies. I'm told I'm too qualified with too much experience or that I have the qualifications and not the experience. Many companies haven't even the courtesy to answer letters.

I've been rejected for being over-qualified, under-qualified, too old, not enough business experience, and too much experience! I've tried everything. I usually get on a short list but there's always someone else. We have money crises. No holidays, no presents. Everything that wears out and needs replacing become a major crisis. My young daughter can't understand why I don't get every job I apply for. My wife can't get used to me being at home under her feet. People who have highly paid jobs, husband and wife working, moan about being short of money. They used to amuse me. Now I go out of my way to avoid them. We don't entertain now and rarely go out to friends.

I've now dropped job applications and have tried moving further into consultancy. But absolutely nothing has happened yet.

I've now stagnated. How can I convince a prospective employer that at 41 I can make a radical change? No interviews have come from answering advertisements. Work disciplines become easily eroded, domestic problems become highlighted. This serves as a warning to friends. There is a temptation to take *any* job to rid oneself of the stigma of being unemployed.

I'm still seeking work. I daily apply for advertised jobs, check Job Centres, seek private work, and so on. As yet, nothing. All this hurts so much. I've had so many ideas for changing career but *all* require training. TOPS will give no financial aid.

Being still unemployed is demoralizing almost beyond explanation. No matter how much hard work and effort one puts into correspondence and application forms the rewards hardly justify the effort. You urgently get your job letters in the post, first-class. You can receive replies by second-class mail postmarked up to 4 days after the date on the letter. It's their market. You see jobs readvertised week after week after being told the job had been filled. If only employers could be as honest with you as they expect you to be with them! Only those who have been unemployed can begin to understand the problems and feelings of the unemployed. The longer it gets, the more anxious you become.

I'm reluctantly reaching the conclusion that people of 51 are of no interest whatsoever. I'm about to have to accept a job selling double glazing. After being in a large company for 28 years doing well-paid, exciting, fulfilling, and challenging work, it's difficult to get into a totally different gear. I now just have to look to self-employment.

There is a dearth of vacancies in the travel industry—I've had only four interviews. In applying for interviews I feel at a great disadvantage being 'unemployed' and therefore somehow less suitable than others. I feel trapped here. I've become more inward-looking. With little to relieve the monotony depression increases. I can't afford to go out, and when the chance arises I don't want to go.

I went abroad for a post, but I was unsuccessful. I'm now trying to develop my own business. The need to keep up appearances and morale creates financial pressures. I feel that if this slips I'll fall into an unemployment rut. My friends are anxious to see me involved, purposeful, and enthusiastic.

I now have tremendous financial troubles and sometimes I feel that somebody up there doesn't like me. I've been through a bout of severe depression.

There are some powerful and sad images portrayed in these accounts. Of action demanding more and more personal effort and courage, with nothing but rejection and failure to show for it. Of doing all that seems possible to find a job, but 6 months have passed without any progress. Of the helplessness in realizing that age may be *the* reason for lack of success: an immutable barrier. Some had given up—a virtual defensive paralysis in the light of a seemingly impossible task. The world also becomes reshaped through a hypersensitivity to *others'* success, income, and 'normality'. *They* seem to have an unfair contentedness and privilege.

If perceptions become jaundiced in this way it is not helped by the one-sidedness of the game in which participants find themselves. The dice seem loaded against them. They give so much to prospective employers to receive back evasive or inconsistent replies; or worse, no replies at all. The courtesies of acknowledgements, personalized letters, and fulfilled promises are easily laid aside when it is a buyers' market. This can feel like a twist of the knife to someone whose fate focuses sharply on what comes through the letter box each morning.

One person, who was originally coping quite well with her difficulties, was no longer:

I've now gone through 5 months of intensive work on job hunting—I gave up 5 weeks ago. I've nothing to show for it, but a few interviews and wasted energy. I've tried everything from kitchen work to professional jobs. I'm sickened that my medical record is probably being used against me. It seems to be OK to be a housewife. Before I declared this there were strong expectations that I *should* be working. But now my husband has to take the burden and his chances of a job are very small indeed. The situation is most unhappy.

78

There is a contrary picture depicted by four other participants. These were all originally unthreatened by their job loss, and continued to be so, despite being still unemployed:

> I am still unemployed, but I've attended a Training Officers' course and I'm now applying for posts. I've enjoyed being at home, doing the domestic chores while the wife's been at work and listening to my favourite programmes on the radio. I'm certainly not depressed.

> I've done absolutely nothing to find a job since the course. Since unemployment my life has been much more pleasant. I now feel that if you can't cut the cake give up eating. Also take the money and run. My position has now shifted from 'unemployed' to 'retired'.
> (This gentleman was the one discussed earlier, well adjusted to unemployment and now thriving in the role!)

> I'm still seeking work and seem to be getting more interviews. My morale is very high. The pressure of unemployment seems to have fallen more on my wife. Perhaps I survive at her expense. I suppose being self-employed over the past 8 years with varying fortunes, I really don't *feel* unemployed.

> I've generally enjoyed the overall process of job hunting. I've made over 40 applications with a high proportion of first or second interviews. I've had one offer that I refused because of its lack of security. I've maintained an active regime with more involvement in local activities. Family ties have become closer.

One participant who was not feeling threatened 6 months previously was now shifting his ground. He was beginning to feel the threat of rootlessness he had not experienced before:

> Being unemployed after a period of time alters your mental outlook. You feel unwanted, loathe to enter a pub or attend any social engagement. Without a close mental grip on yourself you soon feel an *untouchable*.

The overall stress level may not increase over the 6 months continued unemployment, but our analysis reveals that those who have remained threatened by their job loss show distinct qualitative changes in attitudes and coping. Feelings of failure become more endemic, as does helplessness and cynicism. The aura of the event penetrates more deeply into the family. Defensive withdrawal is more common following the constant frustration of being unable to positively influence one's progress. Time passes slowly. In a period of applying for jobs, anxiously awaiting replies, punctuated with gaps of nothing to do, 1 week can feel like a month. Any rewards from hobbies or pastimes have now faded; they may have provided some solace in the early months, but now no longer. In this sense the chronological period of unemployment is not always too helpful for understanding the *feelings* of time unemployed. For some people 6 weeks feels like long-term unemployment; for others 6 months can pass before they feel this way.

But not all of those remaining unemployed felt so threatened. Some originally saw their job loss in positive, opportunist terms, and still did so after 6 months. Their optimism and self-confidence remained remarkably firm and consistent. Clearly the initial meaning of job loss to the participant has a very strong influence on later coping and adjustment.

Unsatisfactorily employed

The quantitative data indicate that a change for the worse occurs amongst those who have become re-employed in jobs they find unsuitable. Sixteen people comprise this total group.

There seem to be three main reasons for this. Firstly, the biggest shift occurs amongst those who initially felt unthreatened by their job loss. The acceptable or positive face of unemployment has not fulfilled its promise. The new job is inadequate and has not provided the fresh beginning hoped for:

> I've gone into self-employment consultancy charging rock-bottom rates for my work in order to get an entrée. I work a lot from home. Almost every approach to companies for business has failed. Thanks to DHSS I'm not *quite* making a loss! However, the financial effects on the family have been considerable with prolonged, difficult rehabilitation. I've realized that I should have changed career 10 years ago instead of doing it this way.

> After years of self-employment, working for someone else is very strange. All the backbiting and comments about other people is hard to swallow. I don't work as hard now – neither do I take problems home with me. I now feel that this job is going to be a temporary one.

> My present job is *worse* than my previous one in terms of what I do and my job title, although the salary is better. I suppose I now have to see the security of the job as more important than the actual work and prospects.

> I don't feel I've really developed in my job—I'm still shrugging off the stagnation of my last job. I feel less status than my previous job, but I get much more money. I worry about what happens if I get fed up with this job—where then?

For these people the blow to self-esteem and expectations is considerable. There are signs of threat to security, achievement, and ambition which did not exist before; indeed feeling trapped in a situation which was no better than the previous unsatisfactory job.

The second reason is to be found amongst those who were initially not coping well with the threat from unemployment. Their failure to cope was aggravated, rather than relieved, by their new job. A successful solution to their problems had evaded them despite the apparent virtue of obtaining a job:

> I'm working below my educational achievements. My career hasn't developed. The job doesn't suit me—there's not enough to do. I'm encouraged to think well of its security. I just wish so many people wouldn't say 'Well, at least you've got a job!' I've slid downhill fast and can't seem to find a way out. I've lost my self-respect—seems like a continuing chapter of failure. I'm seen as the family failure. It's harder and harder to be realistic about what my objectives are.

> It's depressing—emotionally up and down. I'm more aware of those who continue to succeed while I fail.

> I'm not in the industry I want to be in. I've got a lower salary. I will need to move home, consequently I'll see less of my family.

> I'm so ambivalent about the job. I'm pleased to get it, but reluctant to accept it. I can see that I have conformed to my old pattern for expediency's sake, rather than risk something different. So where has this got me?

> I do some teaching now, but it is only part-time. There's so little to do that my ability to do it is suffering from my depression the rest of the week. It's all so insecure. My need for security has increased. I've felt very isolated which has prevented my mind from working as I know it can. It has even brought me to the brink of insanity.

> The job is reasonable I suppose, but I've had to move with my family. This has added further strain to family life. My wife finds it difficult to settle here and she had to give up her good job. My sons are resentful, holding the move against me, having had to leave behind their friends and family. I'm now *very* uncertain about the future. How will my job affect me and my family?

> I've a lower status and salary. It's a come-down and people make crude remarks rubbing it in—'Sorry you don't like it', 'Is *that* car a professional's?' 'What a come-down!' Well, at least I *am* back in employment—I will now have to seek something to better myself.

> I've jumped from one rut into a very different one. It's a high-status job, but abroad. I'm separated from my family and sincerely believe the UK is the best place to be. Basically I still have deep doubts about my ability.

> Until the promised promotion becomes a reality, my current employment is less than secure. I've less salary but better benefits.

For some of these individuals compromise for the sake of expediency was a bitter pill to swallow. A nice, 'clean' solution to their difficulties had eluded them. Because the new job could not heal previous wounds, bad memories and self-doubts lingered on. They would now talk of the *next* job as their ultimate goal.

The final contributing element to the extra difficulties experienced by this group was expressed by just two participants. Both had initially managed their problems well by actively searching out job opportunities—they were anticipating coping with their respective threats to status and achievement. But they were to be very disappointed by the results of their efforts:

My career hasn't developed—it's gone back 10 years. I jumped into a time warp. No title or status, though salary and security has increased. I certainly feel my job is useless at times.

Contrasted to my military life my job is dirty and noisy. Also I notice a considerable lack of organization in the management team. Unionization inhibits me working in certain areas. It's a treadmill sort of job dealing with *immediate* problems, so there is little potential for future development.

Satisfactorily employed

Those who had 'made it' during the 6-month period comprised the largest single group of the follow-up sample—37 per cent of the total. Seventeen of these had experienced particularly high stress before getting a satisfactory job, so their re-employment was especially satisfying for them. For example:

I've now done what I had to to re-establish my track record and what I've enjoyed most in the past. I'm really pleased to be employed and not worrying about the future any more. The family looks much more relaxed.

I was *so* worried and depressed and I could see no way out. But finally, after about 25 applications, I got a job. Now I'm working again I feel quite happy.

The course gave me the *confidence* to apply and get a job which I'm happy in. PER alerted me to the job, treating me sympathetically.

Now I'm a selling-skills instructor earning £10,000 a year. It's a really enjoyable job. I found the whole process of job hunting fraught and worrying, but after a while I could anticipate the questions which previously embarrassed and frightened me. I could acknowledge my shortcomings and counter with my strengths and abilities.

I've now a job—with which I'm well able to cope, with wide responsibilities and excellent relations with the team. The most gratifying thing is that I'm employed again. Getting up in the morning knowing I've a job to occupy me and a salary at the end of the month. It was *embarrassing* being home all day.

I'm getting on really well—everything is better. I'm proceeding along the same career path as before. While unemployed I had greater peaks and troughs, which really got to me. It also affected my family and friends. I became less tolerant of people close to me.

Now I'm self-employed and I've regained the ability to meet and converse with people.

I've now moved away from the deceit and elusive promises of the commercial world, to teaching. Although lower paid it's much more enjoyable. There's no point-scoring and far higher self-respect.

I was sick and remorseful for 3 months, then I finally reached a point when I stopped looking at the past and looked to the future. My problem was 28 years with one company. I've now got all that out of my system. I've gone into partnership selling engineering components to the trade. I feel *very* much better now. I can look ahead.

I gave up security and a pension for this job, but it fits me well and I'm very happy at it. If only we could fit round pegs into *round* holes redundancy maybe less likely.

The remainder of the group were of relatively low stress after their job loss. This made the passage to their new job a fairly smooth, unfussed affair:

Unemployment didn't affect my life much because I was so busy applying for jobs, preparing for interviews, and thinking of my career.

It was all relatively easy. PER found me the job and I was greatly excited by it. I've masses of energy.

Everything is now as good, if not better, than my previous job. There are excellent prospects. I had slight problems keeping my sights high after initial disappointments, with PER encouraging me to look down the scale. Fortunately I didn't have to.

Now I've got a job considerably better than my other one. I even had *two* job opportunities which made me feel guilty knowing others hadn't had such a chance.

I didn't *like* being unemployed, although I can't say it really worried me. I've now started my own company. Things are improving and I should be successful. Actually I had two firm offers which I refused because they demanded a 24 hour commitment.

I'm employed in a similar position to my previous job. My many applications came to nothing. A chance meeting with a former colleague led to the present job. But all the time I could reflect and make future plans.

I've now moved out of industry into social work. I'm very happy. Un-employment was a good time to reassess everything. My life was enriched. But I always felt it was a waste of talent leaving me on the unemployed list!

I got this job after 5 months. It has better security and pension rights, and will be at a higher salary and status within a year. It wasn't as shattering as it might have been because I saw it as an opportunity to *do* something with my life and look for fresh fields. I studied while I was unemployed, which helped show my son that adults are never finished learning. I'm now quite confident that if this situation occurred again, at whatever age, I'd find myself another post.

I now have a responsible job in a good atmosphere. This gives me satis-faction, despite the lower salary. Redundancy, particularly after long service, is not an easy pill to swallow. You have to be very resolute to bounce back again with renewed enthusiasm.

While some of these participants found jobs very easily, others did not. They would go through the same daunting catalogue of approaches, applications, and refusals that others had done. What distinguished them from their high-stressed counterparts was their ability to cope with these disappointments. Their basic positive attitude towards their unemployment would carry them through; or the level of threat never became so great that they would feel unable to defend themselves. This certainly did not mean that they could not express concern and distaste at their unproductive labour, however this rarely turned into a profound emotional upheaval with its attendant chronic anxiety.

Chapter 9

From Another's Point of View

The struggles and adaptations of the participants rarely took place in a social vacuum. Many had people close by who could share some of their burdens, and prizes. In this chapter we will hear from them. Family members, friends, and others who had had their lives affected in some way through their association with unemployment.

Twenty-two hand-written accounts were received with the follow-up questionnaire. These represented a little over one-third of those participants who responded to the follow-up. Seven concerned the still-unemployed, six the unsatisfactorily employed, and nine related to the satisfactorily employed. However, two accounts from this last group were too brief to be of any use in the analysis.

Let us now look at these accounts in full. Each is preceded by a brief summary of how the participant described his predicament and feelings.

Still unemployed

ALAN   Alan, a man in his late 30s, lost his job as service manager in an engineering company 2 months before attending the course. He was very disheartened by the experience, being asked to resign after just a short period in the job. He had put masses of energy and time into the job, and felt he was getting on really well. The company thought otherwise. The threat to his self-image and esteem was high. Added to this were the worries of coping with a new baby. Several months later he was stressed and depressed, having got nowhere at all with his job application.

His wife comments:

During the period of my husband's unemployment our marriage has completely broken down and divorce proceedings have now been started. How much this has been due to unemployment is very difficult for me to assess as our marriage was already shaky. During the nine months my husband has been out of work all the difficulties we had to start with have been extremely exaggerated. The fact that I had my third baby after a gap of 10 years did nothing to help the situation. The baby, arriving as he did three months after my husband lost his job, caused extra financial problems for us and Alan seemed to take his frustration out on the baby. If he had been in work, I am convinced he would not have lost his temper and hit the baby as he did do on the only occasion he was left to baby-sit. He used to willingly look after the other children with no problems.

As a result of unemployment I have watched Alan change from a very active person, into someone who just wanted to sleep all day, very often not getting up until late morning, then moping around until evening when he would sit and watch TV. He lost all interest in the house and garden and could not get interested in any of the numerous jobs waiting to be done. Alan also became very scruffy in appearance, not bothering whether he shaved or not, and often going three weeks without bathing or washing his hair.

I feel that during this time my role has changed from one of wife to mother, only being required to get his food ready and wash his clothes.

MARY   Mary was single and in her late 40s. She was dismissed from a teaching position because she was 'unable to communicate with the kids'. Her pride and confidence were shattered. Her first reaction was to 'hide away in a corner', avoiding contacts with friends and associates. She was put on tranquillizers by her doctor. She replied to the follow-up after 10 months indicating she was very depressed, having applied unsuccessfully for 80 jobs. She felt a deep sense of failure, but found some solace in her religious faith.

Her vicar comments:

I have known Mary rather better over the last few months than when she first became unemployed, when she was still applying for teaching continuation training. As the months go by the initial 'straightforward' applications for another teaching post in this county have been replaced by many different applications. These include private and state teaching jobs, jobs with firms concerned with food etc, and short term Christmas jobs at very low pay. Mary is middle-aged and has trained, and worked, as a teacher. So whatever aptitude tests say about other jobs being more suitable, lack of training and experience militates against acceptance of such posts. This becomes demoralising as weeks/months pass and Mary is applying for 'any' job, 'any'where. Age, length of time unemployed, and the unsuitability of the openings which come up, seem to form a syndrome. If one is not re-employed in the first few weeks re-employment seems harder to obtain as circumstances label one 'unemployed'.

I have seen this pretty much from the outside—viewing, as I say, difficulties compounding themselves. What is the answer? The present attitude of cheerful perseverance seems to be a good attempt at an answer, anyway!

TIM   Tim was Managing Director of a textile firm—his own business for 12 years. A self-made man, with basic school education, he went from prosperity to eventual collapse in the shrinking market. He took a general management post in a friend's business, which did not work out. All this left him confused, with a mounting feeling of failure as his financial pressures increased. Having been his own boss left him feeling vulnerable in competition with others for jobs. At the age of 43 he had not had an interview for 23 years. After a further 12 months his money crises were acute. He had reached a number of shortlists for jobs, but there was 'always someone else'. He would avoid friends and his confidence was at rock bottom. His daughter and wife found him difficult to understand and to manage.

His wife comments:

The most difficult time was when he was first unemployed and was at home all the time. I don't think he applies for enough jobs but he usually (I am sure quite rightly) points out that he hasn't the qualifications. I feel he is not really adventurous enough in outlook and doesn't aim high enough. I feel *a* job would be better than nothing although I do appreciate that he wants a worthwhile job and something that would give him something to work at. He has recently been doing woodworking and electrical factory fitting to keep himself occupied and which is something he likes doing. I do sometimes feel he would be quite happy doing this sort of thing but in a way I feel it is a waste, and possibly not really fulfilling. But obviously it's difficult to do anything outside textiles without qualifications at the moment when there are so few jobs. I find this very difficult to write as I am so involved and it is difficult to sort out one's feelings. It varies from day to day depending on how cheerful or depressed one is feeling.

I know he does worry about what to do and spends sleepless nights trying to work things out and taking tranquillisers to help him sleep (not every night now but did when first unemployed).

Obviously the best time has been when he was offered a job which unfortunately did not materialise. How he felt so optimistic for two months about getting it I do not know.

I have recently been in hospital and Tim was marvellous while I was there and when I first came home and was unable to do anything. It was most useful having him not working at a regular job, being able to fetch our daughter from school, shop, etc.

I do find lack of money makes life difficult as food, clothes and petrol become more and more expensive. Not being able to go out in the car when one wants to and not going out much at all and clothing a growing daughter. Many of our friends and acquaintances seem to be reasonably well off and although we appreciate that most people struggle these days, one does get a bit fed up hearing people complain about lack of money when they have children at public schools, three holidays a year, etc. Although one appreciates that they do work hard for it. It does become a bit difficult accepting hospitality when you know you can't really afford to return it.

I do feel a bit uncomfortable after a year trying to explain to people why Tim still hasn't got a job. This doesn't seem to worry Tim very much. Fortunately he seems much more cheerful about it all than I do. Although I know he does at times feel depressed about it all and we have a lot of futile arguments and rows.

LEN   Len had had a chequered career, having had 18 jobs since the early 1960s. His difficulties had been complicated by periods of nervous breakdown, with unsuccessful attempts to complete university education (for which he was well qualified academically). Thereafter he had become stuck in a career characterized by generally poorly paid, junior clerical posts. He recognized he was unsuited to the work but somehow he was unable to extricate himself. His competence was constantly challenged, resulting in the job losses. He was fired from his last job after his employers had received poor references on him (subsequent to his appointment). His symptoms of strain were particularly prevalent at the period of his counselling—he was finding it very difficult to get another job with his background, and he expressed a profound self-doubt about the directions he was perpetuating. Six months later he had stagnated, feeling trapped by his past. 'How can I convince a prospective employer that at 41 I can make a radical change?' He was getting no job interviews, felt useless, and found domestic issues enveloping him. His strain level was now even higher, but otherwise he presented a fairly 'OK' image of himself.

His wife comments:

It is pleasant having him at home, though our $4\frac{1}{2}$ year old shows a disguised concern that he doesn't go to work any more. But his days, and therefore the rest of the family's as well, lack any kind of structure. We don't get up at any fixed time, and he stays up late because there is no need to get up early the next day. He has no plan to his days, no hobby that occupies him, nothing that he feels he must work at. Although he is very helpful in the house there is nothing he does for his own interest or for its own sake. Because of this, and because it is difficult for me to maintain or superimpose a daily house routine, the children suffer, I think, from lack of routine and unpunctuality of meals.

One of the bonuses of his unemployment (one which must have been very galling and depressing to him) has been that with Earnings Related Supplement and a larger rent rebate we have been better off. The Supplement runs out this month, and then I think life will be much more taut and arid because we will only manage by constantly robbing Peter to pay Paul and making choices like 1 postage stamp = $1\frac{1}{2}$ lb apples = 2 eggs. That's not meant to sound self-pitying; it's how it becomes.

I suppose the worst period was being pregnant and having him ill and out of work and wanting to start 'entrepreneuring'. The best having him home while our baby is so young, so that they can become really well acquainted.

Apart from the financial aspects, it doesn't worry me that he isn't working. It is terrible for someone to slog at a job they're unsuited to, and get no rewards from (neither job satisfaction nor money). I would worry if he were work-shy, but he isn't—though he may be unemployable in this place and at this time. I don't see my role as urging him into drudgery again—I don't nag about that—I do nag him about his lack of self-imposed discipline, and would quite like to change places so that apart from some household tasks I had so much time to do my own things. I've thought about going out to work myself, but we have never discussed it—my husband finds this kind of role reversal repugnant, I think, and in any case it's not practical with the baby only 8 weeks old.

I've read his questionnaire answers, and was interested in his answers to the stress questions. I think most of his answers fit in with what I see, but some of them are opposite to what is true, or wrong in degree. I find him much more depressed than usual and with stronger feelings of worthlessness, which makes me impatient and antagonistic. It's not his unemployed state that worries me—I don't see it as his fault—either in becoming unemployed, or remaining unemployed—(there isn't any work about), or the prospect of counting every penny—we've survived that before—it's his increasing self-negation, which I think makes him defeatist in his job applications and sets up a vicious circle he is unable to break out of. Giving careers advice in isolation—raising job expectations with no follow-up placing agency—can hinder rather than help people in my husband's position.

DON   Don was 37 and had resigned from his travel job for moral reasons. He found that the deceit and dishonesty of his boss was just too much to bear, despite a strong feeling of pride and concern about the job itself. On leaving he felt a mixture of relief and worry about the future, plus a shattered belief in human nature. This he found particularly worrying. His early forays into the job market were unsuccessful, and it seemed that his last employer could be giving him bad references. Self-doubts arose about the wisdom of his action. After 8 months, and four unsuccessful interviews within his profession, he felt his unemployed status was putting him at a permanent disadvantage competitively. He felt trapped, depressed, and became progressively more inward-looking.

His wife comments:

As the months go by my husband gets more and more pessimistic and dejected. To my inexperienced mind he has been most eminently suited for most of the positions that he has applied for and, with each letter of rejection, his depression deepens. Naturally he feels a failure as provider for his family and inferior among friends. Because of this we hardly ever go out even when the outing doesn't involve spending money. By staying at home he doesn't have to force a cheerfulness he doesn't feel, although on the other hand when we are with relations or friends it's easier to forget our situation for a while.

During the early months the best periods were after my husband had applied for a job when hope and optimism were to the fore. The blackest times were after each letter of rejection. Now, after 15 months of unemployment, we dare not even hope when he applies for a job. Of the two of us I am the most optimistic and I cling to the hope that surely something must come up soon and now that we are in a New Year this must surely be better than the last one.

One of the worst aspects is having to say 'no' to the children and I know this hurts my husband deeply. They have had to learn to do without and we have to rely on our parents to provide most of their new clothes and shoes. I feel that we can never repay what they have done for us and I resent having to feel that way.

Throughout I have tried to remain cheerful and jolly him along but at times the future seems so bleak that it's very hard not to give in to one's emotions and the knowledge that there are over two million other families sharing our situation is no consolation whatsoever.

PAUL   Paul was a forceful man in his late 40s. His unemployment was largely self-imposed in that he had decided to give up a career in politics, and also sell his revenue-earning interests. Beneath his action, though, was an unease about his purpose in life. He had reached a watershed in his career and strongly sensed that there was something else he needed to do—but what, he did not know. He found this lack of clear purpose distressing in that it threatened his strong needs for action and achievement. He could find no specific way out of his difficulties and sought guidance. In the 6 months up to the follow-up he had travelled abroad for a post, which he failed to secure. He felt himself falling into an unemployment rut with the need to maintain 'normal' appearances creating financial pressures.

A friend comments:

Since he became unemployed Paul has appeared to suffer the most from the lack of a clear, challenging objective. This has resulted in a listless approach to most tasks and has created an air of despondency which is contrary to his nature. It has been necessary for him to review his career and outlook on life in order to re-motivate himself. Concentrating his mind on preparation for interviews or job prospects have stimulated his interest, but this has only heightened his disillusionment when he has been rejected.

ERIC   Eric was a 40-year-old graduate engineer who had been made redundant from a large engineering organization. Unlike the previous participants, he felt fine about this and, at the time of his counselling, was happy to improve his employment prospects by taking a postgraduate degree in management. After 6 months he had in fact secured a place for full-time study, and had also made over 40 job applications. He had enjoyed the job hunting and had had one offer which he had refused; because by then he felt convinced that further study was the right avenue for him. He was cheerful and optimistic.

His wife comments:

I feel that we both accepted and approached the situation positively; rather than regarding it as the end of everything we felt that it could be a beginning. We spent a lot of time discussing it, looking from every angle. We were determined not to accept just any job, merely to give some immediate security—and then possibly find ourselves with another problem 2 or 3 years hence, we're too old for such risks. Hence the decision to take the MBA course, with a view to a wider choice of jobs in the foreseeable future— though possibly greater hardship in the immediate future.

I think we were lucky in that my husband did not get into a deep depression, one or two short periods of frustration yes, but nothing serious. My husband organized his time reading, gardening, working in the house, etc. and became more interested in local happenings—and more involved with ordinary 'day to day' family life, which extensive overseas travel had previously made impossible. It has been lovely having him around and rather than his being 'under my feet' it has brought us all closer together.

The course made us realise how lucky we were to be able still to look positively into the future, as it seems some members were completely 'flattened' by their experience. I feel sure that meeting others in the same situation must have helped these people to approach things more positively.

At the moment, we both feel optimistic and want to get started on the MBA course. However, I feel that our next crisis point will be at the end of the course, when, if there is no job, financial pressures will really begin to take hold. These are the most damaging, especially with a young family to provide for. But we'll face that if and when it comes. Meanwhile we must adapt to living apart for the duration of the MBA course, not easy to accept, but we both feel it's the right way at this time.

The worst times were applying for jobs, attending interviews but then hearing nothing. The best times were when we were approaching it together, discussing, sharing ups and downs, I've played various roles—an 'ear', a secretary, a supporter (I'll never lose faith in my husband's ability), showing appreciation for all the extra 'odd jobs' done etc.

The effect on me? Strangely, it has really made me feel more worthwhile. Previously, I'd been merely a 'wife at home', receiving no understanding towards the 'minor' problems involved in family life—especially whilst living abroad with a travelling husband. Determined we'll get through with as little upheaval for the children as possible.

An overview

Shouldering some of the problems of an unemployed person appears as no easy task. As a marriage partner, in particular, it proves to be a situation replete with contrasts and tensions which are sometimes strange and confusing. Through this, though, there is a curious mixture of costs and rewards.

Some of the difficulties are clearly spelled out in the above accounts. A marriage which is already fragile can crack under the extra demands of un-employment—it exaggerates pre-existing tensions. There is the deep frustration and helplessness of seeing one's partner becoming progressively more passive, underutilized, and depressed as rejection after rejection becomes the norm. Trying to create some form of order and pattern in domestic life which has been severely disrupted by the unemployment. Attempting to provide emotional support when one is confused and anxious for oneself, one's role, and one's family. In particular, noticing how children can become victims of escalating domestic tension and their confusion about 'why dad is not working'. This can lead to increased pressures to accept *any* job to bring things into a recognizable form of normality, while at the same time realizing this is the last thing that the unemployed individual should do for his *own* welfare. Managing social life becomes a problem because it often brings expenditure which cannot be afforded, and it also highlights one's differences from those who are in employment. The ubiquitous stigma is felt by the family—it goes beyond the individual who is unemployed.

However, within this grey picture lie patches of colour and warmth. The extra physical help of a partner at home can be readily welcomed. Family members who previously had to make do with a modest amount of the 'bread-winner's' time, squeezed into his busy professional life, now have him full time. So some aspects of family life become more cohesive and richer. No longer, for example, is a baby cared for by just one parent. At its best all this can provide a new and valued feeling within the family—a recasting of roles where the unemployment becomes a joint problem to solve, and where everybody's energy is productively harnessed.

Unsatisfactorily employed

MARTIN Martin was an industrial designer in his mid-20s. He was dismissed from his post, a long affair which dragged him down mentally and physically, severely knocking his confidence and his competence. After a further 6 months he had obtained a job in his professional area, but without the title or status he required. Indeed he saw it as a step back in career 10 years. He felt considerably underutilized and uncertain about his role. Reflecting on his unemployment period he noted how the immediate home life improved, but at the same time other members of the family suffered. Whimsically, but with a certain earnestness, he suggested 'Maybe we should be helped to be *unemployed* usefully, instead of chasing jobs that may not be there'.

His wife comments:

Martin's term of unemployment for us as a family caused no great upset, quite the reverse. The children and myself loved having him with us at all hours. Having the land and animals helped Martin a lot, giving him no time to reflect on his position. He got to a point where if your course had not come along he would have carried on between house and land without any great difficulty. He applied for several jobs in the interim period and was greatly disappointed and disillusioned when several of the firms didn't even bother to reply to his applications.

The course, when he started, gave him another interest and he gained a lot of experience and confidence in himself. He thoroughly enjoyed the time he spent there and would come home and tell me about the day's happenings. The difference was apparent when he went for interviews after the course, securing his present position. I didn't know whether to be happy or sad that he was working again. The relationship Martin and I had built up during the eight months he was at home was very precious and while I was happy that we were once more financially sound I didn't want to jeopardize that in any way. I found the only difficulty of having him out of work for that time (apart from money obviously) was our relatives. The strain of unemployment seemed to fall on his parents and mine and they were constantly trying to find suitable jobs for Martin to apply for. They did not like the stigma of Martin being 'on the dole'. That part did not bother Martin and myself overmuch. What did bother him was the fact that he had had the sack from the job.

On the whole the worst period of unemployment has got to be those first few weeks when getting over the traumatic experience of dismissal. It would be easy for me to say the best periods were during and after your course, while this is true in part, it isn't so on the whole. Once the money position had been sorted out satisfactorily with the Unemployment Department things fell into a good routine with Martin and I working together either in or out of doors. That obviously would not have lasted forever and we were the first to realise that in this way the course and the experience it gave Martin were invaluable. It came at just the right time in the unemployment period, although having said that, I think it would have been effective more or less any time during that period.

ANNA Anna was a young graduate social worker who entered social work with a strong 'people' commitment. However the pressures of coping with the face-to-face situations were very much more than she had anticipated. She struggled for a year in the job, to eventually leave, feeling a deep sense of personal and professional failure. She became very scared of further involvement where she might again fail and be hurt. For 2 years she had been in and out of temporary work. Nine months later found her very unhappy in a clerical job, well below her educational attainments. She felt she had lost self-respect in a continuing chapter of failure, and was finding it virtually impossible to sort out realistic objectives for herself. Her church and friends helped a little.

A friend comments:

I have lived with Anna for two and a half years during most of which she was unemployed or in temporary employment. It is hard to say exactly how much being unemployed has contributed, but for the two and a half years I have known Anna she has suffered from fairly deep depression at which times she feels that she is no good for anything or anyone—which is quite unfounded. She has good qualifications and considerable talent, but as time has passed she has lost confidence which has made it hard for her to obtain a suitable job—and as she has been employed in jobs which do not stretch her, she has lost more confidence.

At times, though, she has been more 'on top of things', usually when she has been given some responsibility at work and when she has felt valuable both in the eyes of friends, people at work and in God's sight.

It has been hard at times, because there have been times when I have just wanted to give up trying to encourage—I've found sometimes that nothing I can say seems to help or convince Anna of her worth. We have found that relationships can become strained unless we are prepared to talk and pray things through together.

Anna found the course useful and came back with more confidence, but this was soon lost after a number of unsuccessful attempts to secure a fulfilling job.

ALEC Alec had an engineering background and had been in business with his father for 10 years. Despite periods of considerable success he found that they were constantly being ousted by bigger organizations. His ideas were often exploited by others, so he felt robbed of personal success. As tensions in the business mounted, he decided to leave to find a new direction and identity. He was then 32. In the 6 months to follow-up he had taken a number of unskilled, temporary jobs, and was now considering two offers of permanent jobs. He found his temporary employment strange and distasteful after self-employment, leaving him little incentive for personal involvement. His struggle for a direction was not over and it was all rather more difficult and depressing than he had anticipated.

His girl friend comments:

I have known Alec for almost a year, during this time he has gone through the misfortune of being unemployed. He could not bear the thought of being paid unemployment benefit. I found he envied employed people, wishing all the time he had a job. He knew what sort of work he wanted but none was available. I felt a tender pity for him knowing that he had several qualifications and he was unable to get a job. I think the worst period we went through was when he accepted a temporary job on a tip site. I know he hated that but to him it was a job. I think we both felt let down this being the only job available. The role I played through this is a very good friend and listener as in the evenings we would both sit and talk of his job and his future employment. I have always taken a great interest in the career he wants and always gone along with his decisions and will continue to do so. The only way this has affected me is to make me feel bitter as I could not understand why a person has to take a job which somebody with *no* education could do.

ANDREW   Andrew's unemployment came about from the natural ending of an army commission at the age of 40. He judged that he could go no further with the army but, having been in such a closed community for 24 years, he anticipated a difficult adjustment to civilian life. He was very unsure about what he could offer to a civilian job. He was financially secure, but this did not temper his anxieties about his new role in life. He managed to obtain a supervisory job 4 weeks after the course, and it was a most salutary experience for him. It was a treadmill, trouble-shooting, sort of job with little future development. Unlike much of his military life it was dirty, noisy, with little evidence of clear organization. Also union constraints were strange and inhibiting to him.

His wife comments:

I can give you my observations of my husband for the eight weeks or so before he officially left the services. Prior to coming on your course my husband didn't quite know what would happen to him, though he felt he would accept 'anything'. When it actually came to it the jobs, money and prospect were not too good at all, and it looked at one point as if he would have to take a considerable drop in wages. This worried him of course, as it did me.

He felt at this point that his previous civilian and military acquaintances were a good source to meet the right people who could give him a good job.

Some of these men I found to be of low intelligence and had jobs they could hardly keep down themselves, and were in no position to help my husband find a job. But my husband was so convinced they would, that I found his attitude towards his family changed quite considerably.

As a trained nurse, I knew what he was going through, and sympathised with him. I felt he was just trying to hold on to the army which after all had been part of his life for 24 years.

However, my husband, having completed your course, decided what he really wanted to do, and in a very short time found a very good job. The job provides him with a good salary, and it's a total change of job from what he has ever done. I feel this is what he really needed to make a clean break, and your course helped him to do it. He finds the job interesting and stimulating. He is happier now than he has been for the last eight months.

IAN   Ian was the General Manager of a plastics company when he was made redundant as 'one of the biggest overheads'. He was then 47. The type of business was his life's work and he was very confused about what his next step should be. Tensions soon increased in the family especially with his wife who worked as a full-time nurse and, typically, arrived home exhausted. He had also had some serious health problems in the past and he feared this would be held against him in job applications. During the period up to his follow-up he had managed to find a job which kept him in the plastics industry, but in a different specialism. However, the main cost to this was a move in home which considerably exacerbated the family tensions. In particular, his wife had to give up her job and his sons lost many of their friends.

His wife comments:

It is a most upsetting sight to see one's own husband amongst the ranks of the unemployed, particularly when it has been thrust upon you out of the blue. To see someone that you are so close to, who had given their heart and soul to their job, even to the extent of putting their job before us in many cases, to be put in such a position. It makes one lose complete faith in society and what it is supposed to stand for.

The worst period, after the initial shock, is to help the person maintain confidence in himself as an individual because of the endless amount of rejections in the job market, and the endless amount of applications that are posted off with no subsequent reply. The best period, naturally, is when the answer is 'the job is yours'—the biggest morale booster one can have in this depressed age.

I found my most important job was really to keep my husband's morale boosted, but naturally this in due course also affects you, because it is so difficult for you when you feel so utterly dejected for your partner and the rest of the family. I personally have become very bitter because of the situation as I have had to give up the house which was my ideal and, because of movement to another area, the job of work of which I was very proud. A consolation for all this is that at least by sticking it out together one is absolutely sure that one has a very sound marriage.

PAUL   Paul had been with a foods organization for 12 years as their Sales Manager. He valued loyalty and was very bitter to find himself effectively demoted and then redundant as the company reorganized. He was in his early 50s and he was worried that he would be too old for another post. Furthermore his experience was totally in the area of foods. The only job he could eventually secure was as a sales representative in a stationery organization—an enormous drop in salary and status. His wife wanted him free of the selling pressures, with more time to enjoy home life. He, though, was very keen on a more demanding job.

His wife comments:

My husband was very distressed when made redundant after so many years. At first he did all the decorating all through the house and helped with the gardening. But once the jobs at home had been done he became fed up. At last, after many applications, he started this job which is not very good pay—but as long as it was a job rather than being unemployed it was better than nothing. My opinion is that I loved having my husband at home and really missed him after being here for about four months constantly. Financially we are alright and our house is our own and we have no children, so I would have liked him at home all the while, but I think he missed meeting so many people. I don't think he is really happy in the job he has as it is so different. The trouble was at his last job he was always so willing that they kept giving him different positions until there was no job there. Perhaps it would have been different if he had stayed as a rep.

An overview

These reflections highlight a number of features which emerged from the previous observations; in particular the delight at having a partner at home during the unemployment. The benefit of this was greater for some observers than that of the prospect of re-employment. Yet their ambivalence was knowing, at the same time, that their partner *wanted* to return to work.

We also see how difficult it can be to provide emotional support when feeling dejected and concerned about the family ramifications of the job loss, and also getting little positive reward for one's existing efforts at support. It seems, at times, a thankless task. This was sometimes mixed in with feelings of anger and bitterness because of the perceived unjust treatment of a loved one—capped by the humility of compromise in taking an unsatisfactory job.

All of these participants were disappointed with their new jobs. But it was not always seen in this way by the other person. Martin's wife and Anna's friend make no mention of it. Alec's, Ian's and Paul's views are similar to their partner's. Andrew's wife, on the other hand, sees her husband's job as fine and satisfying for him—very different from his own views. It may be that some people, after re-employment, find it difficult to declare how they really feel about their new commitment; perhaps partly to protect their spouse from further disappointment, but also to protect themselves. An open statement of disaffection can reinforce feelings of failure. It could also be that, in the absence of the day-to-day closeness of interactions which characterized unemployment, they will no longer feel it legitimate to express their self-concerns and doubts.

Satisfactorily employed

TERRY   Terry had had many jobs, all in self-employment, but few giving personal satisfaction. He felt like a butterfly, drifting around and never settling. He was now 32 and was anxious about his aimlessness. He had practical/technical skills, but was not very qualified on paper. He had recently tried to obtain a management qualification, but had failed the examinations. It seemed that the counselling gave him the confidence and inspiration he needed to break his inertia. He secured a senior sales position, a 'clean' job which appeared to give him the stability he sought.

His wife comments:
When my husband was first unemployed, back in December 1978, we both looked upon it as a chance for him to gain some employment in a field in which he was really interested, which would be clean (unlike his previous occupations) and regularly paid—this was the problem when he had his own business. He had the promise of a place on a management course which could lead to various things, we had a regular and sufficient amount of money entering the home thanks to the DHSS, and my husband was able to get on with jobs around the house and was quite happy.

He failed the exam at the end of the first term of this course and suddenly as a consequence of this his spirits fell to a very low ebb. The Job Centre sent details of a particularly revolting grotty job (which fortunately he did not accept), the jobs that he had started on around the house didn't get finished and he was getting very fed up with the world. He considered taking one or two factory jobs but was put off by the smell, noise etc and really felt he was wasting his life.

And then the fairy godmother came along in the shape of your course which really boosted his confidence and taught him the tricks of the form-filling trade, and when he saw an interesting job advertised in the local rag just after your course had finished he had the confidence to apply and the confidence to tackle this job which was on different lines to the one he had had before. Prior to going on your course he would not have had the guts to even apply for it, let alone think that he could do it satisfactorily. I suppose that's the feeling of rejection that being unemployed gives you.

ANDY   Andy's marriage collapsed while working overseas as an engineer. This shook him deeply and it took him some 12 months to adjust to his new role. The attendant problems forced him to resign his job, and he had been filling in time on various temporary jobs which were 'great mental therapy' for him. At the time of the course he was confident and optimistic about the future, and keen to enjoy life and a new job. He obtained a senior executive post within 3 months and was ebullient about its scope and prospects.

His fiancée comments:

In retrospect, Andy's unemployed status seems relatively short-term; but endless when he was actually experiencing it. He had time to experience a gamut of emotions associated with being unemployed—perhaps the most profound of which was that of isolation, in the sense that ultimately the situation can only be resolved by the individual and by his own efforts.

Over the period he was unemployed I endeavoured to offer consistent, empathetic support, while personally experiencing feelings which echoed very much those of Andy himself. Andy feels he would like to have been offered more advice over this period—I was wary of offering advice (the field of engineering is alien to me), and I considered an emotionally supportive role to be more appropriate.

The course was offered in the initial phase of Andy's search for work—its value was not only in offering advice in the practical skills of securing a suitable post, but also in offering Andy the opportunity to clarify and resolve doubts of 'worth' and competence. The course reduced Andy's feelings of isolation and also emphasised the need to pursue a new job in a positive and purposeful manner.

'Worst' periods were those coping with feelings of disappointment, frustration, uncertainty and a generally impecunious state! 'Best'—positive assessment and feedback from course staff and colleagues, and the successful acquisition of a stimulating and rewarding job.

PAM   Pam could not wait to get out of her job in an advertising organization. A big redundancy programme had created a sour, tense atmosphere which she hated. Although over 50, she *felt* very much younger and was keen to find a new job. When the redundancy came her feeling of relief was immense and she threw herself into job hunting. Soon she found that she *could* get interviews, despite her age, and she shortly had two good job offers. She took one of these—a position in advertising with greater scope, independence and security than her previous job.

Her husband comments:
My wife was unemployed for quite a short time, even if one adds to it the period during which she knew she was to become unemployed. Unemployment had little apparent effect on her, apart from increasing the spate of job applications. She clearly had complete faith that she would soon find a job at least as good as that she had lost.

My role in the matter was to admire and encourage, nothing more.

My wife's unemployment, being so brief, had very little effect on me, as I had the good fortune to have a job at the time.

SIMON   Simon lost his job as a Sales Director in late career. His company was failing and contracting fast, so his services were 'dispensed with'. He felt he should have seen it coming, but he did not. He was fairly philosophical about his position, but concerned about the influence it was having on his wife. After 5 months with no job in sight she felt very insecure, and was not sleeping properly. He had initially worked very hard at finding a job, replying to around 150 advertisements and writing to 50 local companies—but with no success. Being nearly 60 years old did not seem to help. Eight months on found him just about to start self-employment. This was his final life-line, but one that appeared right for the situation. He had bought premises for his own manufacturing business and was eager to start.

His wife comments:
Obviously the initial shock and gradual dawning of what it meant in real terms was a bad time. Because my husband is a very complete person I did not have to boost his confidence, nor hide my despair. It did not occur to either of us that he would not get another job, and I was prepared to move and almost convinced myself with every interview that he would probably be better off. After his birthday, obviously 57 sounded much older than 56, he was not offered one more interview, or short-listed. He attended courses and I was grateful that he could keep everything in perspective. More than that, I was amazed that he could be optimistic, that it might have led to a job, and that being a reserved person he could 'bare his soul' filling in questionnaires so honestly. We originally decided to give six months to job seeking in earnest and then risk all in starting up in our own business. That was our worst period. That was *real* insecurity after 33 years of marriage.

The 'savings' would go—the car sold for a small one—I started applying for jobs so that the housekeeping would be covered—maybe raise a loan on the house and be really frightened.

The best periods we hope are to come.

VINCENT   Vincent was a man in his mid-30s who was trying to establish a sales career for himself in the UK after returning from some years of working abroad. His initial attempts, however, had been decidedly unsuccessful. Within a few months he had been dismissed from a sales management post because he had 'not brought in sufficient business'. This left him shocked and drained of self-confidence. At the time of his counselling he had made a few applications for sales jobs, but was very apprehensive about the wisdom of his action. Two months later he had managed to find himself a comfortable niche by moving off the front line to instructing in his professional field. He was happy about the performance and security, but with still some lingering bad memories about being unemployed.

His wife comments:

My initial reaction when Vincent first lost his job was a feeling of tremendous compassion. I suppose I *really* felt needed and that was a good feeling. I felt very close to him. I was relieved that the last job, in which he had been very unhappy, was over. We were helped by his company's kindness in lending him a company car and paying him for two further months. The fact that they wanted him to stay in the company, though not in sales, was very good for morale and helped his feelings of 'loss of face'.

At first, Vincent pottered around at home—that was fine for a while. He looked at ads—half heartedly. He didn't really know what sort of job to look for. He rewrote his CV and applied for various jobs. I remember feeling most irritated that instead of applying for several, he'd wait (and wait!) for a reply before applying for anything else. He became apathetic, irritable with the children (something he'd not been before). He sat around a lot—this started to irritate as there were lots of jobs to do—yet I understood how he felt. I was very lucky in that I was given an incredible peace about the future (I am a Christian) and that 'all would work for good'—but despite *knowing* all would be OK—I felt the job wouldn't drop out of the sky and he'd have to find one!—and he wasn't looking very hard.

One of the difficulties about Vince being at home all the time was interactions with female friends during the day. Our conversations were different—it was a strain in a way. I used to go out to friends a lot during the day—that helped me to share my feelings and I got great support. I felt Vince was not as lucky in this. Often he couldn't share—but when he did we grew closer. I know he felt I neglected housework—and I did!

I was really bothered when he started to grow a beard! Somehow this made it all 'tatty'—I was helped when a friend produced a sticker with 'Love is—letting him grow a beard if he wants to'—it helped me to accept him as he was!—and brought back my sense of humour!! A silly incident, but relevant.

Vince played a lot of squash at this time and I believe that was really helpful. He was a top player for the club—very good for his ego.

He went on the Career course and after this he became much more positive. I feel this course changed his attitude to himself—somehow his feelings of self-worth were very low and I couldn't boost them (that made me feel inadequate). The course was fantastic from all our points of view.

When he came back he tackled applications much more positively—went to a lot of trouble researching etc. Taught himself to type (I'd done it for him before).

Another bad time was when he'd received an application form for his present job. He'd sent a good letter and CV—but kept the form at home for weeks—couldn't manage to write 'how do you see your career to date?'—I remember being very upset with friends one morning—and one of them said 'but he only needs ONE job Jan'. That afternoon a telegram came for him to attend a first interview(despite them not yet receiving the form!). He got the job—as Sales Instructor in Training Dept. I'm delighted because Vince's skills are his gentleness with dealing with people—he's not aggressive enough for actual sales—and he's doing well.

COLIN For Colin redundancy, after 40 years working, was like a breath of fresh air: the first time he had been able to 'take stock'. He was in his mid-50s when he found his job in exporting was to be one of the victims of his company's rationalization. They offered him another post equivalent to that of a clerk, which he found quite insulting and unsuitable. He felt financially secure, but realized that he had never really enjoyed his job—he had just 'done it by habit'. His hobbies and interests were his main joy in life. He found other jobs closed to him because of his age, but to his delight he managed to secure a part-time post in local government which involved dealing with people problems—something he had missed so much in his previous administrative post. His salary was considerably less now, but this was more than compensated by the satisfaction he received from the job.

His wife comments:
After the initial shock of being made redundant, my husband took it in his stride and decided to make the best of things. He fully realised that redundancy at his age was a serious thing but was always confident that everything would turn out right.

He kept extremely busy during his six months at home and caught up with all the things he had been meaning to do and never had the time. I might add that the money he saved us in labour costs alone quite compensated us for the loss of his salary.

He thoroughly enjoyed the residential course he attended, which convinced him of the type of employment he was seeking—which I might add was totally different to the work he had been doing, and which he had never enjoyed.

He was, in a way, fortunate in that he could afford to wait until the appropriate job vacancy came his way but upon seeing the advertisement for the local government position he knew that was what he was looking for, applied for it and was appointed.

Upon reflection I would say that the experience of redundancy, being out of work, and attending the special course gave us both an opportunity to really think and I consider that we have benefited from it. My husband now thoroughly enjoys his job and consequently is a happy man, which, naturally, makes my life a much happier one too.

DANIEL   Daniel felt he had failed in his design job by not creating a department which would survive the redundancies in the organization. There was a long build-up to the eventual decision to lose 700 jobs in his company, a period of extreme uncertainty for him. This was his third redundancy, which added to his fears and feeling of failure. He was relieved when all the uncertainty was over, but this left him with the problem of trying to decide what job he *should* have. He was scared of again taking on something which could be beyond his capacities.

At the time of his counselling he was making job applications but feeling very uncertain about his aims. Home life was more difficult—he could not get used to swapping roles with his wife, who worked full-time. In 6 months, however, he had solved his difficulties. He had managed to get a job where he could use his aesthetic ability and it was less pressured and less 'measured' than his previous job. This freed him to spend more time with his family.

His wife comments:

My husband had been made redundant twice before this last redundancy so the practicalities of getting our finances organized did not present us with problems. This time was different to the others from a financial point of view because I now work full-time and earn enough to just keep us. This took some pressure out of looking for another job I think and enabled Daniel to do some re-assessment—your course being part of that.

However the financial worries are not the whole story as far as re-dundancy or any kind of unemployment goes. This period of redundancy/ unemployment/new job has been the worst—that is understandable on two counts. Unemployment as a whole is much more of a problem than a few years ago and *no-one* can presume they will get another job.

But the other part is much more personal. The job Daniel had been in was demanding and difficult and he was not happy there. In one sense the end of the job was a relief but it had drained him of confidence and left him in a low state of mind. At first he was just angry about the loss of the job and then the self doubts set in. This mood of self doubt affects not only the person's approach to working but their total view of themselves. The longer out of work the deeper this mood becomes however hard or consciously the person works against it. I should think this state of mind affects many people, not just my husband.

As a partner it is difficult to know how to behave. One wants to be as great a support as possible and because of this sometimes one acts unnaturally saying or not saying the things one normally would. I'm not sure how helpful this really is.

These problems are not entirely solved by a new job either. For that presents challenge and adjustment the effects of which are felt at home. Also the loss of confidence may happen to a person in his or her new job. For quite a while I feel Daniel lives under the threat of this job vanishing too. It usually takes 6–12 months to settle properly.

However this last redundancy has had major benefits. Daniel has been successful in his 'self-assessment' and has learnt a lot about himself and others. Once again your course was very valuable. He talks problems out far more than he did before which usually means the problems diminish to the point of disappearing or the solution presents itself. This can only be a useful lesson to have learned.

Finally may I say that my only criticism of courses of the type you conducted is that they do not reach everyone. For everyone who finds themselves out of work through no fault of their own needs help to put the pieces back together again on much more than just a financial level.

An overview

A satisfactory job does not appear to have dulled people's memories of the unemployment period. These accounts accentuate, on the one hand, the progressive debilitating effect that joblessness had on some participants. Their partner's *knowing* that they were lonely, sinking, unrealistically waiting for a reply to one application—even irritated for what they saw as self destructive, isolationist behaviour—but being unable to find a way to help. On the other hand, it can be the partner who felt the more distraught, wondering at the other's calm acceptance of events. The meaning of the job loss was again a relevant factor here—it could be a positive opportunity for the participants, but at the same time a source of threat to the partner.

The jobless period can appear interminable, while chronologically it is relatively short. The empathy portrayed in some of the accounts reveals a long and anguished time up to re employment—and sometimes beyond. There can be a legacy of uncertainty which affects all family relations into the new job period. Is it all going to happen again?

It is noteworthy that, whether or not there was a social upheaval in the aftermath of unemployment, the ultimate benefits *can* be considerable: such as a wife feeling wanted and appreciated in a way she had never experienced before; such as testing out one's religious beliefs and marriage, and finding them sound; and, in particular, learning more about oneself, one's partner, and what one should value in life. The drastic life change precipitated by unemployment can force attention to these factors in ways in which the more usual routines of work and leisure rarely permit.

Courses and care

It is clear that a number of observers saw the course coming at just the right time to provide a much-needed boost to a participant's self-esteem; perhaps providing something that the partner could not. The peer group on the course has been mentioned as important, as well as specific course interventions. These views accord with participants' own recollections. Yet the 'injection of adrenalin' provided by the course could wear off fast without some reward for new efforts or ideas. Indeed, unrealized expectations *without* continuing support could *increase* threat, stress, and depression.

The programme therefore was very much a two-edged sword, cutting through apathy and self-doubt to increase success in job hunting, or leaving deeper scars following failure. It was possible to reduce, or counteract, this latter effect with successive counselling sessions—but this was available for only a minority of participants. The course was not structured (or sponsored) for active follow-up and continuing help.

This leaves us with the question of where and how assistance is required. We can see that the power of the 'victim' to change things unilaterally is limited. Some through force of personality, circumstances, luck, and sheer hard work fall onto their feet. Others do not. Simply telling them how they can get on to their feet, and supporting them emotionally at one or two points in time, is insufficient. It appears that help needs to be far broader and more consistent. Perhaps someone has to fight for them, to provide access to agencies and networks which can give emotional and practical assistance wherever and whenever needed. This could be an excellent role for a specialized social worker. Such a person could help to bridge the communication gulf which we have seen can occur in a family. Reading some of the accounts leaves one with the feeling 'If only they could have talked to each other about this'. The will may have been there, but the strange and taut situation could strangle communication.

The perceptions revealed in this chapter leave little doubt that the immediate family can play far more than just a reactive role in unemployment. In many senses it is *their* unemployment, not just the jobless person's. So why not programmes, briefings, and other forms of assistance for *them* on *joint* action? In this respect it seems short-sighted that courses of the sort provided for the participants in this study should not be open to the wife or husband. The basic skills of counselling and support could then be discussed, rehearsed, and transferred to the natural setting of the home, a process which could be reinforced by the activities of the social worker or a similarly skilled professional. Furthermore, such a shared event can relieve *mutual* anxieties and feelings of helplessness and loneliness. It provides a common base for understanding about unemployment which should help to promote dialogue and problem solving.

We have, then, derived some notions about support for the unemployed from the way that their spouses have reacted and felt. Let us now turn to the participants' own views of the support they have received.

Chapter 10

Support

One of the questions in the follow-up questionnaire asked participants to comment on the 'moral support' they had received during their unemployment; its nature, its adequacy and its sources. Thirty-two people reported their views.

Support, in the sense of encouragement and assistance from others, was not always required or desired. A few were their own source of support:

> I usually don't rely on others' support—I use my own instinct. My wife usually accepts what I do without questioning.

> I feel better *without* moral support from the family, or others.

> Very little support from others—but it was sufficient because I was too busy to worry about lack of support.

The majority, however, found others' support important and necessary. Twenty-two participants talked of help from a variety of different sources: family members, friends, others unemployed, the local community, the church, ministers of religion and (least frequently) PER. For example:

> Everyone in my village is very kind and supportive. They inform me of jobs, pass me newspapers and give me meals. My religious faith has helped me—I've renewed church attendance.

> My wife stood by me all the way. Remarkable. She put up with my moods and managed on very little money.

> Family and friends were much valued for their understanding. The PER and course gave me practical help.

> Enormous, from everyone. Even offers of holiday homes and caravans.

> My wife was fantastic—understanding and patient.

> Support was greatest from the family. One friend actually arranged a job

106

interview for me! Some people *will* go out of their way to help a friend.

Close family and friends rallied. I found *I* could even counsel others in a similar position.

Support came mainly from my friends who are working wives.

The family tackled the job finding as a team.

The impression given here was that support such as practical advice, a sympathetic ear, a shoulder to cry on, or simply a focus of stability in a very uncertain and lonely time, was crucial for maintaining a direction and focus. It often severely tested family relationships and friendships. For the above people it worked; but for others (12 people) it did not:

Support? None! Platitudes from my friends—'It's going to get worse!'

Moral support can never be sufficient in this situation. My wife has given me more than I had a right to expect. The PER deflate me. I bring them lots of ideas and I'm met with 'I'm afraid, etc. etc . . .'.

I've few friends just when I need friendship so much. People are generally understanding though not helpful. Their realism suggests my age and the general unemployment situation mitigates against my re-employment. This adds to my feeling of isolation.

Only well-meaning clichés—'nothing stays bad for ever', or 'something's bound to turn up'. I don't see how others can know how you feel unless they experience it themselves.

Friends offered financial help and offers of 'I think I could get you in at my place'. I should have felt good but I didn't.

Friends have been of little help just when I need them. The injection of fire from the course still carries me through the hard times. Most support now has to come from within—from gritted teeth and the refusal to quit the hunt.

Mainly from others in identical circumstances. But this can never be sufficient; it merely confirms your personal problems and difficulties.

I don't think most people realize that, apart from the obvious financial burdens, the main problem is isolation. You can't socialize with friends and associates because you've got no money. Just to have someone to talk to apart from wife and children, gives a great boost, often instilling hope and restoring flagging ambition.

All my past contacts from 26 years of work were useless—'I'll bear you in mind' was their stock response. Unfortunately after the first few weeks I received little moral support from my wife. She reckoned we could just survive financially, but I knew I couldn't survive mentally.

> Mainly bland sympathy. I missed close friends, although some new ones emerged. I became the family unemployment 'guru', giving advice to others!

> I was upset by the apparent lack of assistance from those in a position to offer it—and then surprised at their warm reaction when I was successful.

> At times I've been very alone despite some people there to reassure me.

There was a tendency for those still out of work to find support least adequate—perhaps a reflection of the acuteness of their situation.

These accounts give us some insight into the subtleties and contingent nature of support. The type of support required by the unemployed cannot be declared specifically and universally. For some participants the mere presence of a close family member to talk to was seen as adequate, but for others much more was required. This seemed to be determined by, amongst other things, an individual's personal need for others in his coping processes—which varied considerably. Support of an emotional kind was of key importance to some of those who had experienced unemployment as a deep personal failure or loss, and for those who were failing to cope with their threats. But this type of support was less relevant for those who found unemployment a positive and liberating experience. For these people more *practical* support was often required—for example job information and career guidance.

The support desired can vary over time. Thus during early feelings of shock or dismay many wished to be left alone to grieve in their own way. Thereafter a non-directive sympathetic ear seemed helpful for their personal reorganization. Still later on more direct practical advice could be the most appropriate form of assistance. Clearly, it is asking a lot of family members or friends to fulfil these various roles, just at the right time. Few had the knowledge or experience to do so. Few had ever seen their spouse or friend in such circumstances. The pre-unemployment role relationship had not been formed around such issues: they were strange and confusing to the potential supportee (hence the retreat to benign clichés or truisms).

Lack of rehearsal of the necessary support skills worked both ways. Often the participant could not articulate what he wanted or needed from another. Not surprisingly, therefore, he could feel frustrated and disappointed in people from whom he wanted support. This could develop into a self-fulfilling prophecy whereby he defined another as unable to give sufficient support, which in turn probably left the helper feeling unrewarded or inadequate, so he/she backed away. And so the circle tightened.

What did seem clear from participants' accounts was if the immediate family could not provide the appropriate support, the chances of getting it elsewhere were slim. While friends and old colleagues frequently went through some of the motions of support, saying they would or could assist, in practice few met their words with action. This left participants feeling even lonelier, more stigmatized, and ultimately cynical.

Professional carers were rarely sought. Indeed, other than the doctor or a minister of religion, few knew to whom they might turn. In a spiritual sense, those with strong religious conviction could comfortably approach their minister or church for help. The few reports of this were very positive. Less so with medical general practitioners. The doctor was usually consulted only when there were strain symptoms, for which they usually received drug treatment— perhaps tranquillizers. There were no reports of psychosocial counselling.

The main state agency to which all participants were referred (apart from the Social Security office) was PER. The impression was given that representatives of PER had little understanding about the participant's psychological state when they interviewed them. Indeed the willingness and ability to act on any practical advice given seems to be as much related to the style, sensitivity, and empathy of the PER officer as to the nature of the advice. For example, we have already shown that the demoralizing effect of continued job refusals can be a considerable problem for some participants. It could then be an ill-timed (although perhaps well-meant) intervention for PER to encourage a drop in aspirations, or a career switch which was alien to an individual's self-perception. Each can be perceived as a further failure to add to that person's stress and strain. The point seems to be that practical help for the unemployed, of the sort that PER purports to provide, cannot be handled as if the unemployed manager or professional was part of a homogeneous group of people—all keen, stable, and motivated to get a new job. The skills of effective practical support intermingle inextricably with those of emotional support, psychological sensitivity, and a theoretical and working knowledge of how unemployment can affect people.

Much of what participants have revealed about their received and desired support is broadly consistent with the views of their partners, as reported in the previous chapter. The close family (or close associate) appears crucial in its supportive role—it can provide the main haven of warmth and succour for the unemployed. Consequently any resources committed to assisting family interactions during unemployment would be desirable.

Beyond the family there seems to be a big void. Few seemed to know where to turn to or what to do. Little aid was evidenced from the previous employer, other than obligatory financial payments. Not surprisingly, therefore, some participants felt left very much in the cold. They had to stumble across whatever help was around, or learn to do without it. No-one seemed to be rooting for *them*.

There seems to be a place for *unemployment* agencies, centres geared to the spectrum of social and psychological needs of the unemployed. An *employment* organization, such as PER, is in no way sufficiently equipped, or designed, to meet the range of issues which preoccupy the unemployed. There is already a considerable initiative in this direction in the United Kingdom. The Trades Union Congress (TUC) has co-ordinated administrative and financial support in the development of centres for the unemployed across the country.

Currently, over 100 such centres have been set up to advise, assist, and involve the unemployed (Trades Union Congress, 1981). Activities vary considerably, depending upon the scope of resources available. They include information facilities, advice and counselling, education, arts, sports and health programmes, the provision of meeting rooms, and creche facilities. Many, however, are existing minimally on a shoe-string budget.

The TUC centres are open to all unemployed. There is currently no detailed evidence on who actually approaches them. My conversations with centre officials, and the TUC, suggest that they are patronized by some white collar workers, but the bulk of those who go to them, and run them, are 'working class' (usually white males). One local organizer talked of his disappointment at the take-up rate of his centre's resources after its 18 months' existence. He blamed the 'apathy' of the unemployed and his lack of resources to be open full-time. Selbourne (1982) describes a group of community workers, teachers, and trade union activists who have directly resisted the TUC's formulation in favour of a 'people's centre'. To them, the unemployed centre conjured up images of a soup kitchen of the 1930s catering for a separate, alien minority. A place was required where unemployed *and* employed could work together.

The image of the unemployment centre is clearly important if it is to appeal to its potential users. (In this respect it is interesting that none of the participants in this study mentioned any contact with, or indeed knowledge of, a local centre). While some technical staff amongst white collar unemployed will be unionized, many self-employed people and managers will not be. Furthermore it would not be surprising to find them expressing antipathetic views towards the actions of the blue collar unions. Consequently traditional class perceptions might mitigate against them joining in activities which have sponsorship outside their normal reference group.

It may be that an unemployment centre, or equivalent, can embrace blue and white collar workers. Certainly, if one sees it as providing a base for the exchange of skills and entrepreneurial advice then the white collar/blue collar divide seems absurd. It could be, then, that any sense of community and support within the centre is better fostered outside of a sponsorship which can be readily aligned with a particular, partisan, interest. Failing this we are back to the divisive, but perhaps pragmatic, 'executive treatment for the executives' —centres which offer services geared specifically to the white collar unemployed. This would mirror the type of separation which now exists between Job Centres and the PER.

Whatever their political colour or shape, centres for the unemployed seem to be, in principle, a sound conception. Ideally, I would envisage them being served by people who knew about unemployment through special training and perhaps first-hand experience. Organizationally they could be designed to accommodate an interlinking flow of projects and activities, perhaps built upon a cell-like structure. Bureaucratic arthritis could be minimised by making administrative posts temporary and/or rotating with minimum hierarchy.

Appointments could be controlled through the participative membership of the centre.

A clear reach into existing community resources would be important—such as towards social work, marriage guidance, legal services, job agencies, recreation, and education. The credibility and power of the centre would be all the greater if some of these facilities could be home-grown, or adopted directly from the community. This would help to avoid the pawn-like feeling that some of the jobless get after being shunted from one institution or office to another.

Chapter 11

The Stigma of Unemployment

The follow-up survey asked participants to comment on their status as 'unemployed'. What did it mean to them and others? How did it feel?

Every respondent had something to say in this area. The overwhelming view was that unemployment was a stigma. This perception applied as much to those who saw their unemployment as a positive opportunity as to those who felt loss and rejection. The stigma was based on the way they felt they were being handled and labelled by various agencies and groups in society; the feeling that they were treated as second-class citizens, branded as 'inferior' in some way or another:

> The jobless are definitely inferior to employed people. I've frequently *hated* my temporary work. It's insecure but certainly preferable to the dole queue.

> There's no doubt that few people want to know you when you're down and out. This was obvious when I approached contacts. There's certainly a stigma in being a manager who's unemployed.

> One of the most damaging and unpleasant side effects of redundancy is the feeling of being thrust out of a group of society. To be fruitlessly applying for jobs can produce a feeling of sheer hopelessness. If we can have 'allowances', not dole money, there's not quite the stigma.

> *Non*-thinking people were envious of me not having to get up early in the morning. The really bad effect on me was having to report to the local labour exchange every 2 weeks. There you really *did* see the unemployed.

> Being unemployed is definitely second-class. People question your capability rather than the cause. Only the unemployed can really understand this. Even now I'm very cautious about a major outlay in case a similar situation should arise.

You are treated by others as one of the victims of government policy—to be pitied. I had started to see myself as a failure and I'm sure others were thinking the same.

It's like being in limbo, or stateless. I felt disoriented. I *hated* taking unemployment benefit. Felt 'unearned', 'money for nothing', 'gained under false pretences'. I couldn't relax at home. Felt conversation becoming dull and housebound, centred around daily chores. To others I looked a normal married woman 'at home'.

Most people avoided the subject—*they* were more embarrassed. It was sometimes a really demoralizing, horrid experience. It's amazing how, in this economic climate, that people aren't more understanding towards the unemployed. Unfortunately, many don't differentiate between getting the sack and redundancy.

There's a feeling of dishonour which takes a long time to dispel. One is soon overtaken by feelings of rootlessness, and disorientation. I even felt self-pity, and resentment towards those colleagues who have been kept on

Being out of work is dreadful, running from interview to interview. You're manhandled like a shoe in a jumble sale. I got so fed up with false promises and false expectations.

People expect you to feel the way they *think* they would feel if they were out of a job. When I talk about my business failing I'm uneasy—where did I go wrong? I get the feeling that people think I could get a job if I really tried—and I now find myself wondering if this is true. People seem embarrassed when we meet—they avoid the subject. What do I put on forms now—'unemployed'?

Those who've never been out of work can have no idea what it's like—that's why it's so easy to pontificate about what's good for the country. I now imagine people regard me as a layabout—my paranoic guilt complex?

Unemployed implies 'useless'. You're always given the feeling that if you tried a bit harder you wouldn't be unemployed. I feel others see me as either unlucky or as a fool. When employed I get up 5 days a week and relax in the evening. Now I get up and the problems start. Domestic issues can envelop me such that I don't get on with job hunting.

It's a terrible feeling. The greatest thing a person has is their pride, self-esteem and ambition. There's nothing more damaging than to know that you can't *select* what you wish to do and *demand* a fair reward on the open market. It's soul-destroying to finally realize that age closes jobs to you. People tend to pity you, which is horrible.

What does one write where the forms ask for 'occupation'? Anything truthful looks about as dignified as a Chaplin custard pie! I see myself as a failure and I reckon others must think the same. I don't *think* this is paranoia. I see people around mc on £7000–£10,000 salaries and I can't get in £1000 a year. I'm sickened! Poison anyone?

It's a stigma, irrespective of what other people say. It needs more public attention, but it certainly needs courage to have one's name identified in the process. You can discuss it with distant friends, but it's difficult with parents or close neighbours.

I feel like a parasite on society. The State should not provide for me and my family. *I* should. I have the feeling of being second-class, that perhaps all my past achievements were not as good or as successful as I thought. I'm sure this shows in job interviews. I resigned from my job for strong moral reasons. To now have to suffer to this extent for my actions makes me very bitter.

I still try to avoid people, especially on Saturdays and lunchtimes when I might meet people involved in my dismissal. I now really wish I would have taken union advice earlier, rather than soldiering on for 2 years unhappily.

For some people stigmatization was associated with a particular event. 'Signing on' was a frequently mentioned one. The depersonalizing apparatus of claiming 'benefit' underlined their position in society—as receivers rather than givers. The proud had to step down to take 'handouts'. People who had normally controlled their own destiny were now passively and helplessly being processed. In claiming benefit they were literally adding their own signature to their inability to support themselves. Being surrounded by people in a similar predicament simply served to remind them that they had somehow arrived at the bottom of the social heap. The feeling that the money they received was unearned produced considerable discomfort for those imbued with the Protestant Ethic. Indeed some refused to claim their legal due because of their firm belief in providing for themselves.

Completing job application forms also helped to cement feelings of inferior status. The 'job history' section of the form is clearly aimed at employment rather than unemployment. Participants were soon to learn that, all other things being equal, the currently employed applicant tended to be favoured over the currently unemployed. As time out of work increased so did the problem of finding a credible cover story for being unemployed. The catch in which they found themselves was that there were rarely satisfactory forms of explanation for their unemployment which would reduce its negative stereotype. This applied regardless of the reason for job loss. The blemish was intrinsic to the event, rather like the acquitted crimimal suspect who cannot lose his 'undesirable' image. 'When the dung hits the fan . . .', as the quaint old saying goes. There were some ways, however, of looking better on paper, and diverting attention from the unemployment. Becoming a student was one; the respectability of studying, or training to improve one's knowledge and employment prospects. Another was part-time and self-employment, or consultancy. Some participants managed to sustain a variety of these activities while still searching for full-time employment.

The process of stigmatization was a particularly vicious circle for those already feeling they had failed and been rejected. For them the world was bleak, so they were more sensitive to possible discrimination. They, like everyone else, felt different, and usually uncomfortably so. They sensed others' embarrassment at their predicament, which could compound their own. Conversations and social interaction became strained because of the lack of a central anchor in their lives. This missing stabilizer created an uncomfortable vacuum. Family and friends were confused as the familiar reference points were missing. The job had patterned the features of life which formed the social links; now the job had gone ambiguity prevailed. What was there to talk about? As time passed without a job, conversation about this area became progressively more taboo or difficult, like the effect of a malignant illness that is clearly not responding to treatment.

Perhaps most hurtful to participants was the implication that they were not really *trying* to find a job; that their joblessness was well within their own hands to cure if they would put a bit more effort into it. These messages came from a variety of sources—the media, politicians, and unthinking, casual (and close) acquaintances. It was certainly possible that some participants had not chosen the most productive routes to find a job. Nevertheless the energy, and anguish, which they poured into the task was usually immense, quite unlike that that one would expect from a 'work-shy', 'unable' population.

One can offer the unemployed sympathy and pity. One can point out how bad things are in the country, and that many more are going to be made unemployed. And this is just the sort of response that they found so alienating, reinforcing their feelings of helplessness, isolation, and rejection. It accentuated how well off the other person was in relation to themselves. It was also a sign that others had no real idea of their predicament, or of the stigma which such attitudes serve to reinforce.

The legacy

Given the harshness of the experience of unemployment for some, and the stigma which was universal amongst these participants, one might expect some legacy after re-employment—memories, images, fears, and learnings. The following typified the most salient recollections:

I now take unemployment seriously, instead of just another statistic on the box. I've developed a healthy disrespect for the *status quo*. Being on the dole is certainly a millstone around one's neck when trying for a job. Even *in* employment I now find myself trying to explain away this blemish.

I pretended not to have unemployment status, but I felt very vulnerable, angry, and frustrated at the time-consuming bureaucracy and delays in getting a job and state benefits. I don't think I'll ever ignore the unemployment statistics again, and I get very angry at the glib comments made on TV and in the press on the generosity of state benefits and the effectiveness of agencies to assist the unemployed.

I am now *forced* to see the security of the job as more important than the actual prospects.

I still feel I've failed as a person by being unemployed. My job history seems to be against me. Job failure equals personal failure, so who *would* want to employ me?

My previously held firm opinions on the 'right' to work are no longer such. Perhaps I'm more tolerant of other people's individuality now.

The stigma of unemployment is still a reality—even now I feel it.

I now consider unemployment to be increasingly inevitable during a working life. In some ways it has been beneficial in that I shall be more philosophical towards the problem next time.

Naturally I now have greater understanding for anyone I know undergoing the trauma of unemployment.

After the unemployment I still have doubts about my ability.

I'll no longer be a workaholic for a company. I've now declared just what I'll be responsible for and that's that. This leaves me much more energy and time to develop family and leisure activities.

Unemployment is degrading and worrying. It was a traumatic and sobering period in my life. I now realize that there is no such thing as security any more. You have to be selfish. Loyalty to the employer and extra hard work will get you little credit in the end.

I can now see how soon unemployment can affect self-respect, undermining one's confidence. One becomes a shadow, rejecting sympathy, bitter, avoiding friends, physically debilitated, jumpy, haunted, and afraid. I'll never, ever, forget this.

Unemployment is unpleasant. It casts doubt upon one's competence and self-confidence. But it also allows one to appraise one's career and life. I now have far greater understanding for others unemployed.

It's the worst thing that can happen to anyone. Am I ever going to get to the end of it? But it has to be faced. There are so many like me who may be alone without someone to encourage them. That's the way of life.

The status of 'unemployed' is not too bothering in some respects, but it's the DHSS restrictions which destroy any inclination to self-help.

Approximately half of those re-employed made comments of this sort. They exemplify three main themes:

The lasting blemish. Re-employment did not simply remove the stigma of unemployment. The scar remained as a reminder of the stigmatizing event; it was now permanently part of one's 'record'. For some self-doubts lived on through the new job, especially if that job was unsatisfactory. Feelings of having failed as a person still haunted them, with continuing concerns about their abilities.

Attitude changes towards the unemployed. These were of two types: a hardening of views towards unemployment and an increase in tolerance and understanding of the unemployed. Of the former, there was a sharp intolerance of political platitudes about the economic 'need' for unemployment for economic recovery. The *individual* reality behind the unemployment statistics was now known to them, so macro-statements on employment policy frequently appeared hollow, detached, and ignorant of the personal effects of unemployment. Some would feel angry, but powerless. So they would shrug and accept the situation philosophically or fatalistically. None talked of their own involvement in political action to assist the unemployed. They did, however, show sympathy and understanding of the unemployed. No longer, they would say, would they be able to ignore the problems and difficulties of the jobless.

Sub-optimising. One clear legacy of unemployment was increased cautiousness and cynicism. 'If that's what I get for loyalty and hard work, in no way am I going to give of myself like that again', went the argument. Consequently some participants would become more instrumental in their new jobs, doing just enough to survive reasonably comfortably, but giving their employer no more. For the older participants, being in effect punished for their past loyalty was a very bitter pill to swallow. They would now retrench in defence and refuse to put themselves in that position again. Those whose security was rocked by their job loss took care that this was preserved as far as possible in the new job. This could be at the expense of other needs—such as achievement or status. There was a general feeling that commitment to work was inadvisable—they had now been bitten too hard. Altruism was not a recipe for survival; selfishness was. In this sense unemployment had left a pool of disenchanted people—hardly the material for organizational excellence and economic recovery.

The blemished and those who blemish

The process of stigmatization in unemployment bears a close resemblance to the stigma of deformity, character blemish, or race described by other writers. In particular there are noteworthy parallels with Goffman's (1963) analysis.

Goffman states that the stigmatized individual finds that those who have dealings with him fail to accord him the regard that he has learned in other respects to know as 'normal'. Looking at the participants' records, they reveal experiences very much of this type. Many talk in terms of a general change in the way that others evaluate them; a change for the worse. Their 'discredit' is joblessness, imputed in a way which suggests a defect of character. Conversations with familiar people become strained, uneasy, and false—and perhaps censorious. Contacts with officialdom place them in unfamiliar, subordinate roles.

In response, as we have seen from their accounts, the unemployed may avoid meeting people, feel angry, frustrated, and ultimately dispirited. There is also a circularity in the way that some come to view themselves. They may not initially have felt blemished but the outcomes of their interactions have informed them, in one way or another, that they *are*. They are not received by others in accustomed ways. This can eventually lead to a shift in self-image—'Maybe I *am* inadequate—a failure.'

Some participants did not seem to require contact with, or feedback from, others to feel this way. For them there was an *implied* stigma in the act of losing their jobs. The general 'desirability' of work was a very influential part of their socialization and experience. Therefore 'no work' automatically signified being different from, and less adequate than, those who work.

Goffman argues that individuals will attempt to remove their stigma in a variety of ways, in particular by correcting what they see as the basis for their failing. In our case, this would mean regaining employment. But, suggests Goffman, this does not necessarily result in a return to 'normal' status. Rather, it will be a transformation into someone who now has a record of having corrected a particular blemish (e.g. 'Mrs Jones who had a nose-job' or 'Mr Smith who had a skin graft'). The legacy of unemployment described by those back at work is consistent with this view. The traces of stigma live on in their minds. Also their descriptions of the unfavourable reactions they have received from potential employers to any earlier unemployment adds weight to Goffman's thesis.

Engaging in something which is in general inconsistent with, or countervailing to, the 'failing' is seen by Goffman as another stigma-reducing strategy. In this sense participants would undertake *any* form of work, regardless of skill, rather than 'do nothing'. This could be part-time activity or temporary consultancy. Studying also operated in this way, although perhaps not as potently.

During counselling I sometimes wondered to what extent the very course setting and my own 'secure' job could be aggravating participants' feelings of stigma. I, and the course staff, were part of the 'normal' population to which they nominally, did not belong. We did not share their stigma. In practice, though, it appeared that the programme's helping characteristics, its history, and the general nature of intervention research, put all the course staff into a special category. We were not 'one of them', but we were 'wise' (in Goffman's terms) to their situation through working in an establishment which clearly catered to their wants. Consequently we would not evaluate them according to their stigma and they should feel no shame in front of us.

The personal problems of stigma sometimes arose during counselling. While I could not prevent others stigmatizing, I could help participants handle unfavourable evaluations, and introduce a different sense of perspective on self-worth in unemployment. For example many felt swamped by their 'failure'. I was sometimes able to draw their attention to recognizable 'successes' at other points in their career and focus their thoughts on the self-learning which could be *positively* associated with the job loss.

In such interventions I was sometimes left with the feeling that all this was very easy for me to say to them. *I* did not carry their stigma. I could sense it, and empathize, but in the final analysis *they* had to cope with the consequences of it, not I. This was forcefully brought home to me as I read one participant's evaluation of the course in which he said:

> . . . but in the end I couldn't help thinking that you, the staff, would all be going home to a nice, secure situation with a job to return to the next day. Not me.

Part of the answer to reducing the stigma of unemployment must come from those who comprise the other part of the stigmatizing process—the employed. Creating centres which are directly concerned with the range of unemployment problems, bringing together both the employed and the unemployed (as discussed previously), should assist in reducing the apparent oddity of job loss. They should provide some sign of social legitimization for the unemployed. But the attitudes which underpin stigmatization lie very deep within the positive social values associated with employment. At this level we require a much broader diffusion of information and public debate on work and non-work, and in particular, alternative forms of social organization, different ways of sharing wealth, and ways of meeting personal needs. This may come, perforce, as the unemployed figures soar and young people, especially, cannot get work. More desirably though, it should be planned content in educational institutions, and the subject of serious media reports and programmes.

Chapter 12

Stress, Strain, and Self-Esteem: Sample Trends

This penultimate chapter takes a broader statistical view of the participants as they were at the time of the course, using the data from the structured measures. It provides information on the pervasiveness of their reactions to unemployment and offers some explanations of the variations observed. It is a very different form of analysis from the qualitative format of previous chapters, but can be seen as complementary in its aims.

Imposing statistical models on one's data means (a) that the findings tend to be relatively simplistic, lacking the richness and individualism derived from qualitative data, and (b) that the search for an overall statistical trend provides an understanding which talks of 'populations', 'samples', and 'average men', not of individuals. Nevertheless, for many, such analyses provide the comfort of generalizations which help them to make sense of the world. But a word about the nature of such generalizations. In social science, which has relied heavily on demonstrating non-chance statistical differences and associations, we are rarely faced with one-to-one relations. There are, it seems, few laws of gravity in human social conduct. We are usually left, therefore, with a statistical expression of 'modest tendency'. A rough patterning to our data, teasing out that slight something that we all might have in common. Numerically, our statistics are usually very weak in explanatory power or in level of generalizability, leaving more unexplained than explained. Thus, while the correlations of around 0.40 and 0.50 which appear in some of the following tables have some respectability in analyses of this sort, they nevertheless provide no more than a very vague sense of order amongst otherwise disordered or disconnected data.

So, with these caveats in mind, let us look at our sample trends. We shall firstly examine the stress, strain, self-esteem, and anxiety distributions, and their interactions. Thereafter we will look at how stress, strain, and self-esteem are influenced by age, period unemployed, previous unemployment, reason for unemployment (including personal control over job loss), marital status, and sex differences.

Stress

The basic descriptive and comparative statistics for the General Health Questionnaire (GHQ) are shown in Table 4. The instrument picked up the full possible range of stress scores from 0 to 30. Goldberg (1972, Appendix 7) provides some American data which can be used for comparative purposes. It is clear that our sample is significantly more stressed than the two samples of patients on which he reports. However, they are no more stressed than the small group of unemployed managers who completed the GHQ in my previous study (Fineman, 1979).

Goldberg finds a score of 4 or more is highly likely to identify an individual who displays psychiatric disturbance. On this basis 60 per cent of the sample are disturbed by stress to some degree (12 per cent less than I have found previously).

Strain

Of the 18 strain symptoms on the symptom checklist, a maximum of 10 were reported by two people as having caused specific trouble since their unemployment. Forty-four people reported no symptoms. The distribution of strain scores is presented in Table 5. There were no particular trends in reporting certain symptoms more so than others, and no symptom on the checklist was left unchecked.

For the present study any person reporting at least *one* strain symptom has

Table 4   Stress scores and comparisons as measured on the General Health Questionnaire

	N	Mean GHQ	α	t	
Present sample	100	7.43	7.07		
American general practitioner patients (general)	569	3.97	5.44	4.89	$p < 0.01$
American general practitioner patients (professionals)	111	3.65	4.69	4.49	$p < 0.09$
UK unemployed managers (Fineman, 1979)	25	7.20	6.31		n.s.

n.s. = not significant

Table 5   Strain scores and frequency distribution
Strain

	N	Mean	α	Range
	100	1.56	2.15	0–10

Strain score

	0	1	2	3	4	5	6	7	8	9	10	11+
Frequency	44	17	17	9	4	0	3	1	2	1	2	0

been categorized as a strain 'case', so resulting in 56 strain cases in the total sample. Of these, 33 declared symptoms that they had never experienced before. For them unemployment had brought its unique physical costs.

Despite the confidentiality of the checklist, and the collaborative nature of the study, it is possible that some people would feel reluctant to declare certain, or even any, medical complaints. Therefore the strain scores could represent an underestimate of the existing levels of strain in the sample.

Stress and strain combinations

Table 6 looks at the various combinations of stress and strain in the sample. Using the cut-offs previously discussed each person is entered into the table according to whether he was experiencing 'stress' or 'no stress', and was reporting 'strain' or 'no strain'. In this way we find that 26 people are free from all reported symptoms, compared with 42 who have *both* stress and strain and 74 who have *either* stress or strain. This reinforces the earlier argument that stress and strain do not necessarily go together. Eighteen experienced stress, but no strain, and 14 described strain, yet no stress. In correlational terms stress and strain are associated moderately at 0.55 ($p < 0.01$; Spearman rho).

Table 6   Stress and strain combinations

	Stress	No stress	Total
Strain	42	14	56
No strain	18	26	44
Total	60	40	100

Self-esteem

The scoring of the self-esteem scale derives a score range of 0 to 6, zero representing the lowest self-esteem. The pattern of scores is tabulated in Table 7.

The distribution has a high negative skew, approximately half the sample scoring 4 and above.

The only comparative normative data known to the author are those provided by Rosenberg (1965) in his study of adolescent self-esteem in America. The scores from his large representative sample ($N = 2695$) are shown in Table 7. Compared with the present sample, the distribution differs significantly, the differences being most apparent at the extremes. This is amplified by dividing each of the populations into thirds—low self esteem (0–1), medium self-esteem (2–4), and high self-esteem (5–6). The percentages from this analysis are

Table 7   Self-esteem—distribution and comparison

	Self-esteem score							
(Lowest)	0	1	2	3	4	5	6	(Highest)
Frequency	6	5	4	15	17	25	28	
Cumulative percentage	6	11	15	30	47	82	100	

Mean: 4.19; σ: 1.76; range: 0–6

Compared with representative sample of US adolescents (Rosenberg, 1965, p. 21)

	Self-esteem score							Total
	0	1	2	3	4	5	6	
Frequency of:								
Adolescents	34	108	214	425	683	775	456	2695
Unemployed	6	40	4	15	17	25	28	100

$\chi^2 = 30.56$; $p < 0.01$

	Self-esteem category		
	Low (0–1)	Medium (2–4)	High (5–6)
Percentage of:			
Adolescents	5.26	49.06	45.07
Unemployed	11.00	36.00	53.00

shown in Table 7. It appears that, compared with Rosenberg's population, unemployment polarizes self-esteem. This does seem to make some conceptual sense in the light of the influence of the impact of unemployment on self-esteem. The unemployed group is characterized by a split in feelings after unemployment—those feeling good about it (acceptable/positive impact reactions) and those feeling bad (rejection, failure and loss).

Anxiety

The personality trait of anxiety was inferred from the neuroticism dimension of Eysenck's Personality Inventory (EPI). Table 8 gives the basic statistics for the 64 participants who completed the instrument, and the comparisons with norms presented by Eysenck (Eysenck and Eysenck, 1964).

Table 8   Anxiety—distribution and comparisons

	N	Mean	σ	t	
Unemployed	64	10.89	4.70		
Compared with:					
General population*	2000	9.07	4.78	3.05	$p < 0.01$
Professionals*	58	7.95	5.12	3.30	$p < 0.01$
Managerial*	83	8.06	4.83	3.58	$p < 0.01$

* As presented by Eysenck and Eysenck (1964).

Eysenck finds that managers and professionals are generally the most psychologically stable of occupational groups; it is therefore particularly noteworthy that the unemployed are significantly *less* stable than the very large (2000) general population sample, *and* the smaller sub-groups of professionals and managers.

Could it be possible, then, that the low stability of this section of our sample somehow contributed to their unemployment? This is an intriguing question and rings of Social Darwinism—that the more unstable are less fit to survive at work. We have little existing evidence on this type of issue. There is one unpublished study by Hartley (1979) which compares the scores of unemployed managers with employed managers on the Sixteen Personality Factor Questionnaire (16PF) (Cattell *et al.*, 1970). She found no evidence of unemployed managers being 'less well adjusted' than employed managers. Using the 16PF in my previous study of unemployed, there was no overall tendency to anxiety when compared with the normal population.

So the small amount of evidence we do have suggests that the less stable are no more prone to unemployment. But the above studies do not use the EPI, so it is possible we are revealing slightly different aspects of stability in the present group.

The reader who is predisposed to believe that this unemployed group's relatively low level of stability made them more likely victims for unemployment needs to address at least three further points before resting comfortably with this conclusion:

1. It may be that PER are biasing their selection of candidates towards the visibly more anxious. The anxious people will appear to be in more need of direct help.
2. Despite the claims for the EPI being a situationally independent measure, it may, nevertheless, pick up more localized responses to the unemployment experience. It could be, therefore, partly a measure of stress. There is a moderate correlation between the EPI and GHQ (Spearman rho$=0.41$; $p < 0.01$) which is consistent with this possibility. Although the correlation might, of course, mean that the more anxious people will report greater stress.
3. If greater anxiety increases one's probability of being unemployed, why should this be so? Are more anxious managers and professionals less competent? Less able to run a business? More likely to create interpersonal tension? The link (if there is one) appears obscure.

Interrelationships between stress, strain, esteem and anxiety

Some of the associations between measures have already been mentioned. Table 9 brings them all together. Rank correlations have been used in preference to product–moment correlations because of the non-normality of the self-esteem and strain distributions.

Table 9   Interrelationships of stress, strain, self-esteem, and anxiety

	Stress	Strain
Self-esteem	–0.58	–0.48
Anxiety	0.41	0.44
Stress	—	0.55

Note: All $Ns = 100$, other than anxiety which is based on $N = 64$.
All correlations are Spearman rho.
All correlations are statistically significant: $p < 0.01$.

They are all moderately sized relationships, even allowing for the fact that some artefactual association is possible when different perceptual measures are completed in one 'sitting'. (Actually a number of participants did not do them in this way. They spread the 'load' across the whole period of the course, handing in their completed documents before leaving). Summarizing, the relationships appear as follows:

1. the higher the experienced stress, the lower the level of self-esteem;
2. the higher the level of strain, the lower the level of self-esteem;
3. the more anxious one is, the more one is inclined to report stress or strain;
4. there is some tendency for highly stressed people also to experience strain.

The correlation coefficient is an index of association—not of cause. Therefore the choice of emphasis or direction in interpretation depends on the partiality of the researcher and any guiding theories he is using. Consequently, we can add to the above statements in a number of different ways by using our stress framework. Hence it follows that self-esteem will be depressed by the experience of stress, but also low self-esteem will exacerbate experienced threat, and any consequent stress. The same patterns are possible with strain.

The findings for anxiety fit with our expectations that this particular personality variable will help to trigger stress and/or strain. Furthermore the stress–strain link is consistent with the view that one can develop a stress–strain cycle where one's awareness of personal strain increases feelings of stress, which in turn manifests itself in further strain. Worry, leading to an ulcer, leading to more worry, is a syndrome exemplifying this.

Age effects

Age, in no overall way, directly affects the experience of stress, strain, esteem, or level of anxiety. All the correlations in Table 10 are near zero. The personal effects of unemployment were no more burdensome for the old than for the young.

Table 10   Age—Stress, strain, self-esteem, and anxiety

	Stress	Strain	Self-esteem	Anxiety
Age	0.03	0.00	0.12	0.02

Note: Spearman rho correlations.
All correlations statistically insignificant.

Period unemployed

Is longer unemployment generally more corrosive in its effects? The correlations in Table 11 show that it has no overall effect on stress or self-esteem. It has a tiny influence on strain. These results suggest that it can be naive to view increasing length of unemployment as resulting in progressively deteriorating

Table 11   Period unemployed—stress, strain, and self-esteem

	Stress	Strain	Self-esteem
Period unemployed	0.00	0.18*	0.00

Note: Spearman rho correlations.
   * $p < 0.05$.

mental health—the types of adaptation that occur during the lengthening time are probably crucial for understanding this point. It may be, however, that significant deterioration only occurs beyond the time-range tapped in this part of the study.

Whether or not adaptation to strain follows a similar path to stress is unknown, although it has been earlier suggested that the physical resistance properties of susceptible organs of the body will vary between people. Consequently, as time passes certain people will begin to experience strain that they had not encountered earlier on. Such a time effect seems to be very slightly evident across the sample.

Previous unemployment

Does previous unemployment make the job loss more or less personally damaging? Is it viewed as another indication of personal incompetence, lack of worth, or poor credibility on the job market? Or does it inure one to the stress and strain, perhaps by providing one with skills at coping with the situation?

Table 12 compares the stress, strain, and self-esteem findings on the 26 people who had encountered previous unemployment with the 74 who had not. Statistically none of the mean scores differ. Thus it seems that previous unemployment makes one no more *or* less personally vulnerable. It is as if each new unemployment is a fresh, unique problem or challenge.

Reason for unemployment

Coping with unemployment—and resultant stress, strain, and feelings about oneself—may plausibly link with how the unemployment came about. For example, more personal difficulties may arise in coming to terms with a dismissal than a voluntary redundancy.

Table 13 shows the mean scores for stress, strain, and self-esteem for each of the four main reasons for unemployment. The patterns emerging are similar. Those who have been dismissed or made compulsorily redundant show more stress, more strain, and have a lower self-esteem than those who volunteered for redundancy or resigned. But it is only the stress results that are statistically significant. The remainder have occurred by chance.

Table 12   Previous unemployment—stress, strain, and self-esteem

Stress

	N	Mean	σ	F
Previous unemployment:				
Yes	26	8.35	7.37	0.587 n.s.
No	74	7.11	6.99	

Strain

	N	Mean	σ	F
Previous unemployment:				
Yes	26	1.38	1.86	0.232 n.s.
No	74	1.62	2.25	

Self-esteem

	N	Mean	σ	F
Previous unemployment:				
Yes	26	4.15	1.80	0.015 n.s.
No	74	4.20	1.75	

Control

When discussing why they had lost their jobs, the notion of how much *control* they had had over the nature of the decision and its timing frequently arose as something of importance. This seemed especially crucial for those who were used to controlling their own fate and making their own decisions. The control notion seems to fit with our data. If we assume that being dismissed or made compulsorily redundant means little-to-no control over one's job loss, we can then separate those people in these two categories from the rest who have some control over their predicament. This analysis is presented in Table 14.

The mean scores for stress, strain, and self-esteem all discriminate in the anticipated direction, sharply and significantly for stress and strain, but a chance difference for self-esteem.

We can conclude, therefore, that one of the reasons behind the variation in reactions and adaptations to unemployment could be rooted in how the job loss had come about, and in particular in the amount of control an individual had over the process. The effects of such control are most noticeable in its reflections on stress and strain, rather than on self-esteem.

Table 13   Reason for unemployment—stress, strain, and self-esteem

Stress

	N	Mean	σ	F
Dismissed	22	9.45	6.63	3.15 $p <0.05$
Compulsorily redundant	39	8.87	8.06	
Voluntarily redundant	5	3.40	3.44	
Resigned/left	34	5.06	5.69	

Strain

	N	Mean	σ	F
Dismissed	22	2.27	2.71	1.70 n.s.
Compulsorily redundant	39	1.69	2.19	
Voluntarily redundant	5	1.00	1.22	
Resigned/left	34	1.03	1.66	

Self-esteem

	N	Mean	σ	F
Dismissed	22	3.86	1.96	0.78 n.s.
Compulsorily redundant	39	4.05	1.88	
Voluntarily redundant	5	4.40	1.51	
Resigned/left	34	4.53	1.50	

Marital status

Does the 'natural' supportive structure of a marriage act as a buffer to the negative effects of unemployment? Or perhaps responsibility for others serves to exacerbate stresses and strains? These fairly gross, but different, hypotheses can be examined in Table 15.

While the mean differences in stress and strain are slightly lower for the married people, this is but a chance difference. It seems that marriage does not materially reduce or increase the stress and strain of unemployment in this group.

What it does do, however, is to relate to feelings of self-esteem. It appears that those who are married have significantly higher self-esteem than those who are not married. Thus it is possible that marriage can bolster an individual's self-confidence after unemployment in a way that is denied to a single person.

Table 14   Control of unemployment—stress, strain, and self-esteem

Stress

	N	Mean	σ	F	
Control	39	4.85	5.45	9.24	$p < 0.01$
No control	61	9.08	7.53		

Strain

	N	Mean	σ	F	
Control	39	1.03	1.60	4.08	$p < 0.05$
No control	61	1.90	2.34		

Self-esteem

	N	Mean	σ	F	
Control	39	4.51	1.48	2.19	n.s.
No control	61	3.98	1.89		

Male/female differences

Finally, let us examine whether or not unemployment differs in its effects across the sexes. Again it is unclear what difference, if any, should exist. On the one hand one could argue that the loss of job to a male is a symbol of his particular failure in our society (especially if he is a breadwinner) in a way that a female is unlikely to experience. On the other hand a female attaining managerial or professional status is still a fairly rare phenomenon, so losing one's job after surviving perhaps considerable competition and prejudice may be very stressful.

Table 16 shows the mean stress, strain, and self-esteem scores for males and females. No significant differences exist. We conclude that males and females in this sample are not differently affected. Clearly, however, on a statistical basis we are confined to comparisons with a very small group of females.

Brief overview of the sample trends

Putting the various relationships together we can gain some overall summary picture about the stress, strain, self-esteem, and anxiety of the group as a whole at the period of their counselling. The more noteworthy trends appear as follows:

Table 15   Marital status—stress, strain, and self-esteem

Stress

	N	Mean	σ	F
Married	65	6.88	6.82	1.14 n.s.
Not married	35	7.51	7.51	

Strain

	N	Mean	σ	F
Married	65	1.48	2.26	0.276 n.s.
Not married	35	1.71	1.95	

Self-esteem

	N	Mean	σ	F
Married	65	4.48	1.59	5.17 $p < 0.05$
Not married	35	3.66	1.94	

Stress and strain

Sixty per cent of the sample are disturbed by stress to some degree, a similar proportion to those reporting strain. Forty-two per cent are experiencing both stress and strain symptoms.

Neither the age of participants nor their period of unemployment shows any marked effect on stress or strain. Previous unemployment does not increase (or reduce) susceptibility to stress or strain.

How they were made unemployed does seem important in their overall reactions (a rather different statistical finding from the influence on initial impact reported in Chapter 5). In particular stress is greater for those who had been made compulsorily redundant or dismissed, and both stress and strain are more severe for those who appeared to have little control over the circumstances of their job loss.

Self-esteem

Self-esteem tends to be polarized amongst the group. We find relatively more people feeling very positive or very negative about themselves than is evident in a broader comparative population group.

A low level self-esteem is associated with greater stress and strain. It is likely

132

Table 16 Sex differences—stress, strain, and self-esteem

Stress

	N	Mean	σ	F
Male	82	7.66	7.26	0.473 n.s.
Female	18	6.39	6.22	

Strain

	N	Mean	σ	F
Male	82	1.43	2.02	1.76 n.s.
Female	18	2.17	2.64	

Self-esteem

	N	Mean	σ	F
Male	82	4.23	1.76	0.255 n.s.
Female	18	4.00	1.78	

that self-esteem will both reflect and influence stress and strain levels.

Self-esteem seems to be better supported in a marriage than out of a marriage, but a marriage does not reduce levels of stress and strain.

Anxiety

Part of the group was 'abnormally' high in their level of trait anxiety, which in turn probably contributed to higher levels of stress and strain. It may also have contributed to their job loss, although why this should be is unclear.

Chapter 13

Summary—and Speculations

Bringing together the major points of our analysis, the following picture emerges of the lives of our 100 unemployed white collar workers.

1. The impact of their job loss was by no means a uniform experience. It could be felt as a sign of rejection or failure, the loss of something particularly valued, or as an acceptable or positive experience. These different forms of impact particularly reflected the type of bond which existed between the individual and his previous job.

The majority of participants were intimately attached to their jobs such that job loss was felt as a considerable loss or slight. These people expressed shock and despair at what had happened. They had high levels of stress and strain, and a depressed self-esteem. This symptomatology was also characteristic of those who had had early failure experiences in the job market. But, by way of contrast, a substantial minority had little affection for their previous jobs. The impact of job loss for them was one of relief, release, and sometimes unbridled optimism. Their self-esteem was high and their stress and strain low.

2. Over two-thirds of the participants were considerably threatened by their job loss. Unemployment attacked core elements of their selves, leaving them vulnerable to stress. Most apparent was the threat to pride and confidence, competence and self-worth, security and purpose, and identity. There was a very powerful image presented of the job satisfying these fundamental needs in a way which no other existing social institution could. This would also be reflected in non-work roles which had previously been carefully attuned to the work role. Family life, hobbies, and other social patterns soon failed to function effectively—they only 'made sense' in relationship to work. Generally speaking, without the job it was difficult to relate meaningfully to anything.

3. Threat was not a universal experience. One-third of the group did not feel

133

under attack. Two reasons were behind this. The first was that job loss opened specific opportunities to *meet* unfulfilled needs. The previous job, far from satisfying important needs, had left them wanting and frustrated. This *reactive* low threat was rather different from the response of those who we have termed *proactive* low threat. These people were forward-looking in their views. The past job was immaterial to the future—and the future looked good. A new job was 'just around the corner'.

4.   There were clear psychological and physical costs associated with failing to cope with threat. High stress, strain, and low self-esteem were amongst these. Failure after direct action to obtain a job had become synonymous with failure to cope with threat for many of the participants. Their job seeking had been characteristically energetic, methodical, and flexible—yet in vain. Desperation and despair would soon follow. Constantly unrewarded effort frequently led to chronic self-doubts and anxiety, feelings which were exacerbated as family and other social relationships began to disintegrate. It could also lead to apathy and a disengagement from the job search process. There seemed little point in continuing to hunt in such a hopeless situation.

5.   A number of individuals were overwhelmed with the threat that their job loss had precipitated. Handling these anxieties dominated their reactions. They had not attempted to grasp their difficulties in a more confronting way: they were too tense and confused to do so. Their defensive withdrawal had, how-ever, become difficult to maintain. Many could still see what was threatening them and recognized that they were not effectively coping, yet they had no idea what to do or where to go. Their stress and strain bore witness to this.

6.   Some had coped well with their threat by anticipating success from the actions they had already taken, or were about to take. The failure syndrome had not engulfed them—yet. Indeed, their level of confidence and optimism provided good armour against the immediate threat. Others coped by re-construing their situation—carefully examining what was threatening them and coming to terms with their fears and anxieties.

7.   The 6-month follow-up study provides evidence on changes which have occurred amongst the group. Prominent amongst these was the marked increase in difficulties for those who felt unsuited to their new jobs. Their stress, strain, and self-esteem were worse than when they were unemployed, and also worse than those who were still unemployed. Indeed continuing unemployment appeared to consolidate existing levels of stress, strain, and self-esteem rather than aggravate them. On the other hand, finding a suitable job results in a clear drop in stress and strain and a considerable elevation of self-esteem.

8. Being still unemployed after a further 6-month period hits hardest those who were originally threatened by their job loss. Cynicism, helplessness, and defensiveness increase, as does family disruption and insecurity. Yet their disaffection was qualitatively *less* poignant than those who felt unsatisfactorily re-employed. The let-down was enormous for those who had anticipated a fresh challenge in life, but in fact encountered little that was new or exciting in their job. They were experiencing threats now which were not there originally. Others had acted swiftly and 'successfully' in attempting to remove the threats from their job loss, only to find that the new job did not meet their expectations or needs after all. They had failed, and now felt the consequences in terms of bitter disappointment and stress.

9. Half those who had found a satisfactory job were experiencing high stress before their success, so they were particularly relieved and delighted to be working again.

10. Perspectives form a participant's spouse, or close friend, reveal a two-sided picture. On the one hand there is the considerable pressure which falls upon the partner in trying to support what often seems a desperate, if not lost, cause. In feeling powerless to help someone admired or loved. In attempting to maintain a 'normal' personal and social life under economic stringencies, and under the shadow of the unemployment stigma. Family members can feel the confusion in identity and purpose as much as the unemployed. Habitual routines are thrown into disarray and the strength of the pre-existing relationship is severely tested. Some collapse. On the other hand there is a surprising silver lining for some. Partners effectively forced to re-evaluate themselves and their relationships for the first time: a *meaningful* role for a spouse who had been previously more of an appendage to another's professional career; the mutual caring for children; and ultimately the satisfaction and joy of seeing through a crisis, and coming out stronger and more self-aware. It is perhaps a particular irony that it should take unemployment to precipitate such important self-learning.

11. Support from others seemed critical in the adjustment and coping process of the majority of participants. For a number of people the much-needed support was either not forthcoming, or insufficient. It was complexly interrelated with the existing social patterns in the potential support network (usually family and friends) which frequently failed to meet the unusual situation. Neither the helper nor the participant knew what to do, leading to mutual frustration and disappointment. Or what they did do was inappropriate for the circumstances. The nature of desired support varied considerably, depending particularly upon the impact of the job loss, how threatening it was, the form of coping, and the self-reliance of the participant.

12. Despite the apparent growing social awareness of unemployment, the participants all felt a stigma in being unemployed. It was associated with considerable shame, degradation, and inferiority. Such was the intensity of these feelings (and for some the threat which accompanied their job loss) that a sour legacy remained after re-employment. Feelings of failure persisted and a number of people talked of ways of guarding against a recurrence of this by minimizing their commitment to their new job and organization.

13. A statistical examination of the total group reveals a high incidence of stress and strain, a polarization in self-esteem, and a high average level of anxiety. Neither previous unemployment nor age is related to stress or strain, but the control participants had over the circumstances of their job loss is significant—the more control the less the negative reactions. A marriage can help to support self-esteem, but does not seem to attenuate the levels of stress and strain.

Some impressions and speculations

Working with the unemployed who have been described in this book, and seeing certain facets of their life unfold, has left me the disquieting feeling that the function and meaning of employment has become unnervingly central to our social and psychological integrity. We start (say the economists and politicians) with the economic necessity for employment. The job then happens to become the focal arena for meeting more basic psychological needs such as emotional security, achievement, and a sense of competence. This in turn determines how our family and social life is organized. And then it can all be stripped away for reasons once more 'economic'. Thus the quality of life is precariously dependent upon a specific economic employment system which we serve. There is no alternative presented. One is educated and socialized to 'earn a living'. A non-worker is viewed with concern. He is a 'deviant'; a 'parasite'.

But a number of things have gone wrong with the economist's blueprint. Firstly, as revealed by our study, the structural reshaping to 'revitalize' an economy which results in unemployment is not always met by similarly 'healthy' human restructuring. Not only can people become socially, psychologically, and physically sick in such circumstances, but the scars of the illness can remain. Thus the potential re-employee has changed. Indeed, maybe he does not want to be an employee again. He really is *not* just an 'economic unit'.

Secondly, the employment setting itself can prove debilitating, even to the managerial and professional worker. As the only acceptable setting to earn his living he can find that he gets no more than just this for his many years of effort. So, at worst, the days and years of his working life are passed in a type of psychological vacuum. He can become stultified because, for one reason or another, the job cannot meet its latent (but incidental) functions. He is far from a fully active, excited organizational member. He can turn to non-employment settings to meet his needs. This may or may not work out. Most leisure activities exist in *relationship* to employment. As such they are not intended as employment substitutes and the social norms governing participation in them have grown up in terms of a complement to, or even compensation for, work. There are views expressed that leisure is the reward for working. Formal employment should not be expected to be need fulfilling—it is a means to other pleasurable ends. This seems a perverse logic and one that is rooted in the Protestant Ethic. It is also a convenient rationalization for maintaining work organizations which owe their design and purpose primarily to the industrial engineer and macroeconomist. People have to 'fit in'. In a sense they do just this—but not without considerable cost.

At its best employment can be deeply satisfying and challenging. This applied to around 20 per cent of the participants in the study—surprisingly few for a managerial and professional group. More were attached to their organization for security reasons, and even more were there under sufferance.

Perhaps the ultimate trap, or confidence trick, in the employment/unemployment adventure is that re-entering the employment system is not based upon some clear neat equation of worth against which a jobless person can assess himself, and be assessed. He is at an automatic disadvantage given the blemish of being made unemployed (for whatever reason). He is viewed as suspect if he wants to change career (even though jobs in his occupation may now be virtually non-existent). He is seen as particularly odd if he wishes to go *down* the hierarchical ladder. His older age, which may have once spelled security and status, is now viewed as a handicap. Added to this he is likely to be sorely unpractised at the skills of obtaining a job. Interviews, application forms and CVs can seem like a world apart. Domestically he may be far too established to 'be mobile', as his government exhorts him to be. To be mobile can finally erode a mature network of family and friendship patterns which has already been strained by the job loss. Serious retraining and education look nice in theory, but will it really help in the end? It is an enormous risk if it does not, especially given the financial and psychological barriers to overcome to make relearning possible.

With luck (hard work is certainly not sufficient) a jobless person can gain from unemployment. As we have seen, some of our participants have moved into very satisfying jobs which meet needs which have been frustrated for many years. Without luck there is no job or perhaps a job worse than the previous one. In these circumstances unemployment reminds us that there is no alternative to employment (and here I include self-employment) which is regarded as a socially acceptable form of self-representation. Consequently, without a clear alternative an individual feels 'personless'. There is nowhere else that he, or others, would recognize as a viable setting to exercise his skills and meet his needs. Also, of course, there is nowhere, other than a job, that he can earn money to buy what he cannot produce himself. It is perhaps significant that none (save one) of the unemployed in the study conceived of any alternative to re-employment. Even a 'bad' job was seen as better than none at all. The employment response is deeply embedded in our social repertoire.

Blaming the victim?

If people become trapped in employment, whose fault is it? If they are judged as 'incompetent' and lose their jobs should they not bear some responsibility for this? It is easy to depersonalize problems and blame the 'system' for all evils, as if the particular hurt individual was not part of this system. So, in theory, a person is responsible for his own decision to join a particular work organization, and for the way he performs in that setting. He can, in principle, lobby, pressurize, argue, and help determine his own fate. He has the *potential* to carve out his own destiny. On this basis one might argue that those who 'succeed' in employment are more likely to include the politically acute, the self-reliant and the interpersonally skilled.

But the end-state of this sort of argument is 'blaming the victim' for his 'incompetence' (Ryan, 1971). Somehow it is *his* fault if he cannot 'make it'. He should have *known* to be more politically active, more intelligent, more able, more stable, or whatever. He should not have taken the job in the first place—his bad judgement. This twist of the knife neatly absolves others from blame. It ignores a host of influential processes. For example, that career decisions are rarely neat and rational (e.g. Speakman, 1980). Many people do not know what to do and stumble across an occupational niche. Information on careers, and guidance towards them, is frequently *ad hoc* reflecting school streaming at an immature age, parental confusion (or dogma), social class and opportunity, and the occupational myths embedded in our culture. The selection process into a job may mirror the selector's prejudices and naïvety, compounded with those of the candidate's. The 'qualifications' for entry can bear little resemblance to the qualifications for competence and survival. The latter are only discovered after getting into the job—and by then it might be too late to do much about it. Development and coaching within the organization may be casual, or non-existent.

So an individual's employment and unemployment cannot be cleanly separated from the social and structural forces which have shaped them. Of course some people will be better equipped for survival, and through self-endeavour, taking and creating opportunities and risks, will mould satisfying jobs and careers. But it is an arrogant society which views this as evidence of the worthlessness, or incompetence, of those who have not 'succeeded'.

It is hard to resist the conclusion that some of the reactions described in this book portray one of the devastating consequences of a society where people, like things, are valued in terms of their use. As other writers have observed (e.g. Gouldner, 1969; Fromm, 1947) people are tradeable in a market economy and come to evaluate themselves according to their market value. To be 'successful' accords high value; to fail renders one useless. Like a failed product, the unsuccessful worker is dispensable.

Whither change? Whither help?

Looking at the current social and economic policies enacted in the United Kingdom, and in other Western democracies, there is little to suggest that the viability of the market economy is being seriously questioned. Indeed, in the United Kingdom the shape of the rules of the game remains alarmingly static. Getting people back into employment is the unquestioned goal, and 'create jobs' is the naïve slogan. (In psychiatry this might be described as neurotic fixation).

There is little evidence of politicization by the unemployed white collar worker (similar to the position of the blue collar workers of the 1930s). I heard no loud cries for social change from my participants. It seems that the energy that can be mustered following job loss is devoted to maintaining self-integrity, possibly coping with stress, and *individually* seeking a new job. Self-protection and family protection are paramount, and this is all done quietly, privately. The stigma associated with job loss no doubt mitigates against self-publicity and collective action (as does the belief in the transience of the situation).

The policy of the Trades Union Congress (1981) is clearly against separate unionization of the unemployed. Their desire is to encourage the voice of the jobless inside of the existing union structure (a stance which they presume will provide a more united front for the protection of existing jobs). The plausibility of such a policy to the unemployed would likely depend partly upon the esteem in which the existing union is held, and also upon how well it fought for the protection of the previous job. Given that it ultimately failed, this may not be too good a starting point for enthusiastic membership. However, no doubt some of the responsibility for the job loss can be legitimately deflected elsewhere.

Despite the TUC's predilection, a few independent unions for the unemployed have emerged in the UK. The attraction that these have for white collar workers is not known. One might anticipate more of a blue collar than white collar affiliation, although the desire to unionize is probably initially more a matter of the social and psychological appropriateness of such activity to the unemployed.

The existence of an organized unemployed population comprising skilled, and generally articulate, individuals could represent a powerful voice in pressure for social change, if they wanted change. There is little evidence from the participants in this study that they had thought much beyond the technicalities of getting another job. Speculations on different social formats seem to have emerged more from people outside of the unemployed population (e.g. Pym, 1981; Jenkins and Sherman, 1979). A report from an 'Employment Think Tank' (1979) raises some interesting possibilities in this arena. They propose an economy based upon 'activity' rather than jobs, including the considerable development of non-economic activity which would be creative, or just plain fun. Central to such thoughts is the fostering of self-fulfilling time-structuring occupations to meet the social and psychological void which job loss can leave. 'Wealth' could be differently allocated as fewer people earn money, perhaps through skill-bartering. New patterns of work could evolve centring upon the family (rather than its separation as now), while job-sharing and sabbaticals could become more common.

Less-grand designs for amelioration of the difficulties of the unemployed have already been discussed. The unemployment centre, in particular, seems to offer scope for activity, innovation, and psychological support, plus a modest antidote to stigma. The machinery (e.g. schools, universities, and the media) is there for influencing more positive, constructive attitudes towards unemployment and the unemployed. It now needs to be harnessed to such ends.

But all this is prospective. There is still the dreadful helplessness felt by some of the unemployed. This book did not set out to be a self-help manual; nevertheless there are some basic, concluding, messages embedded in the findings appropriate to self-help:

1. Support from others is important. For emotional support immediate family and friends can be crucial. But this can be as strange a process for the unemployed person as for the helper, so links with people outside the family—counsellors, social workers, ministers of religion—may be necessary. Job hunting can be planned and executed as a joint venture with the family or with trusted friends. Practical support should be sought from reference libraries, advice bureaux, employment agencies, and consultants. Also courses on self-presentation and interviewee skills can be useful.

2. Stress is often reduced through relaxation and exercise. Appropriate routines should be regularized. Strain symptoms should be reported to a physician.

3. Ways of filling time with job-type activities should be sought. Consultancy, part-time employment, self-employment, or charitable work are possibilities. (Hobbies and leisure interests may soon lose their lustre and appeal). Job hunting can be treated as a job of work on a 9 a.m. to 5 p.m. basis.

4. Careful thought should be given to what is wanted out of work and life; a similar *opportunity* may never arise again. Maybe the old career is not the only possible route. Career guidance and counselling might help. The temptation to take the first job that comes along, whatever, should be resisted. This could stack up worse problems and disappointment for later on. On the other hand *any* job may provide a springboard to a good future job, if it is viewed in these terms.

5. Getting work is unlikely to be easy. Rightly or wrongly, the unemployed are 'blemished', and at an automatic disadvantage. Faced with the low

availability of jobs in a recession all routes possible should be tried. Friends, ex-colleagues, the back door, the side door, and the front door. Many dozens of applications are typical of this process. 'Friends' may soon prove disappointing. 'Cold calls' should be made. It is not advisable simply to wait for advertisements to appear. Lots of irons should be kept in the fire.

6. Further education and training might be worth considering, especially if grants are obtainable. Educational settings can open job opportunities through their own networks and they will also provide a respectable 'home' from which to approach potential employers.

Appendices

Appendix A   Strain questionnaire

Below is a list of specific medical complaints. Have you been troubled by any of them since your unemployment, or at any time before then? Please circle around 'yes' or 'no' as appropriate.

Complaint	Caused trouble since unemployment?	Caused trouble before unemployment?
Skin complaint (e.g. eczema, rashes)	Yes/No	Yes/No
Asthma	Yes/No	Yes/No
Chest pains	Yes/No	Yes/No
Back pains	Yes/No	Yes/No
Heart problems	Yes/No	Yes/No
Dizzy spells	Yes/No	Yes/No
Headaches	Yes/No	Yes/No
Migraines	Yes/No	Yes/No
Stomach upsets	Yes/No	Yes/No
Ulcer	Yes/No	Yes/No
Arthritis	Yes/No	Yes/No
Diarrhoea	Yes/No	Yes/No
Diabetes	Yes/No	Yes/No
High blood pressure	Yes/No	Yes/No
Dryness of mouth	Yes/No	Yes/No
Difficulty in breathing	Yes/No	Yes/No
Hot and cold spells	Yes/No	Yes/No
Numbness and tingling in arms and legs	Yes/No	Yes/No
Any other complaints (please specify)	Yes/No	Yes/No

Appendix B

Table B1   Impact—Stress, strain, and self-esteem
Stress

	Rejection/failure $(N = 42)$	Loss $(N = 23)$	Acceptable/Positive $(N = 35)$
Mean	11.19	7.26	3.08
σ	8.08	5.11	3.55

$F = 16.77; p < 0.01.$

Strain

Mean	2.29	1.52	.71
σ	2.52	1.53	1.69

$F = 5.59; p < 0.01.$

Self-esteem

Mean	3.59	4.17	4.91
σ	1.80	1.72	1.48

$F = 5.92; p < 0.01.$

Table B2   Impact—trait anxiety

	Rejection/failure $(N = 31)$	Loss $(N = 12)$	Acceptable/positive $(N = 21)$
Mean	12.06	12.92	8.00
σ	5.06	4.34	3.03

$F = 7.04; p < 0.01$

Table B3   Impact—reason for unemployment

	Dismissal	Compulsorily redundant	Voluntarily redundant	Resigned/ left
Rejection/failure	10	20	0	12
Loss	5	9	3	6
Acceptable/positive	7	10	2	16

$\chi^2 = 9.22$ n.s.

Table B4   Impact—age and time unemployed

	Rejection/failure (N = 42)	Loss (N = 23)	Acceptable/postive (N = 35)
Age (years)			
Mean	42.0	40.8	41.9
σ	8.74	9.33	9.48

$F = 0.58$ n.s.

Time unemployed (months)			
Mean	7.12	5.72	6.41
σ	9.22	7.77	8.60

$F = 0.20$ n.s.

Appendix C

Table C1   Stress and threat

	Stress			
	N	Mean	σ	F
Not coping with threat	55	11.84	6.56	44.65 $p < 0.01$
Coping with threat	12	1.83	2.08	
Not threatened	33	2.12	2.58	

Table C2   Strain and threat

	Strain			
	N	Mean	σ	F
Not coping with threat	55	2.29	2.33	8.16 $p < 0.01$*
Coping with threat	12	0.83	1.03	
Not threatened	33	0.61	1.63	

* Because of the irregular distribution of strain scores this finding was checked non-parametrically. A similar, strong relationship emerged ($\chi^2 = 24.35$; $p < 0.01$).

Table C3   Self-esteem and threat

Self-esteem	N	Mean	σ	F	
Not coping with threat	55	3.65	1.70	6.90	$p < 0.01$
Coping with threat	12	4.42	1.73		
Not threatened	33	5.00	1.56		

Appendix D

Table D1   Follow-up—stress

	N	Mean	σ	F	
Still unemployed	17	7.71	8.56	6.56	$p < 0.01$
Satisfactorily employed	28	2.07	3.80		
Unsatisfactorily employed	12	9.75	9.45		

Table D2   Follow-up—strain

	N	Mean	σ	F	
Still employed	17	1.35	2.21	5.90	$p < 0.01$
Satisfactorily employed	28	1.11	1.75		
Unsatisfactorily employed	12	3.75	3.36		

Table D3   Follow-up—self-esteem

	N	Mean	σ	F	
Still employed	17	3.76	2.05	10.55	$p < 0.01$
Satisfactorily employed	28	5.29	0.85		
Unsatisfactorily employed	12	3.17	1.75		

Table D4   Follow-up—age

	N	Mean	σ	F	
Still unemployed	17	46.65	7.24	0.85	n.s.
Satisfactorily employed	28	42.86	10.65		
Unsatisfactorily employed	12	38.76	9.42		

Table D5 Stress change

		Mean		σ		
	N	Initial*	Follow-up	Initial	Follow-up	t
Still unemployed	17	7.00	7.71	6.62	8.56	-0.44 n.s.
Satisfactorily employed	28	5.93	2.07	4.83	3.80	3.91 $p < 0.01$
Unsatisfactorily employed	12	7.91	9.75	9.24	9.45	-1.60 n.s.

* The initial means do not differ significantly between the sub-groups.

Table D6 Strain change

		Mean		σ		
	N	Initial*	Follow-up	Initial	Follow-up	t
Still unemployed	17	1.59	1.35	2.00	2.20	1.07 n.s.
Satisfactorily employed	28	1.32	1.10	2.06	1.75	0.69 n.s.
Unsatisfactorily employed	12	2.33	3.75	2.84	3.36	-2.16 $p < 0.05$

* The initial means do not differ significantly between the sub-groups.

Table D7 Self-esteem change

| | | Mean | | σ | | |
	N	Initial*	Follow-up	Initial	Follow-up	t
Still unemployed	17	4.23	3.76	1.30	2.05	1.52 n.s.
Satisfactorily employed	28	4.53	5.29	1.48	0.85	−3.00 p <0.01
Unsatisfactorily employed	12	3.92	3.17	1.83	1.75	2.28 p <0.05

* The initial means do not differ significantly between the sub-groups.

References

Aitken, M., Ferman, L. A., and Sheppard, H. L. (1968). *Economic Failure, Alienation and Extremism*. University of Michigan, Ann Arbor.

Argyris, C. (1980). *Inner Contradictions of Rigorous Research*. Academic Press, New York.

Arroba, T. (1979). The social and psychological aspects of redundancy: to what extent a problem? *Personnel Review*, **8** (3), 25–9.

Beer, N. F., and Swaffin-Smith, C. (1976). Rejuvenating the redundant manager. *Personnel Management*, **8**, (12), 26–9.

Berthoud, R. (1979). *Unemployed Professionals and Executives*, vol. XLV, p. 582. Policy Studies Institute.

Blumer, H., (1969). *Symbolic Interaction*. Prentice Hall, New York.

Braginsky, D.D., and Braginsky, B. M. (1975). Surplus people: their lost faith in self and system. *Psychology Today*, **9**, 68–72.

Cattell, R. B., Eber, H. W., and Tatsuoka, M. M. (1970). *Handbook for the Sixteen Personality Factor Questionnaire (16PF)*. Institute for Personality and Ability Testing, Champaign, Illinois.

Cavan, R. S. (1959). Unemployment—crisis of the common man. *Marriage and Family Living*, **21**, 139–46.

Cobb, S., and Kasl, S. V. (1977). *Termination. The consequences of job loss*. National Institute for Occupational Safety and Health (NIOSH), Cincinnati, Ohio.

Daniel, W. W. (1974). *A National Survey of the Unemployed*. PEP, London (vol. XL, Broadsheet 546).

Eisenberg, P., and Lazarsfeld, P. F. (1938). The psychological effects of unemployment. *Psychological Bulletin*, **35**, 358–89.

Employment Think Tank (1979). *Unemployment—A new Approach for the 80's*. The Institute of Employment Consultants, London.

Estes, R. J. (1973). The unemployed professional: the social, emotional and political consequences of job loss among education workers. Unpublished doctoral dissertation. University of California, Berkeley, California.

Estes, R. J., and Wilensky, H. L. (1978). Life cycle squeeze and the moral curve. *Social Problems*, **25** (3), 277–91.

Eysenck, H. J., and Eysenck, S. B. G. (1964). *Manual of the Eysenck Personality Inventory*. University of London Press, London.

Fagin, L. H. (1979). The experience of unemployment II. Unemployment and family crisis. *New Universities Quarterly*, Winter 1979/80, pp. 66–74.

Fagin, L. H. (1981) *Unemployment and Health in Families*. Department of Health and Social Security, London.

Ferman, L. (1964). Sociological perspectives in unemployment research. In A. Shostak and W. Cromberg (eds), *Blue Collar World*. Prentice Hall, Englewood Cliffs, NJ.

Fineman, S. (1979). A psychosocial model of stress and its application to managerial unemployment. *Human Relations*, **32**, 323–45.

Fink, S. L. (1967). Crisis and motivation—a theoretical model. *Archives of Physical Medicine and Rehabilitation*, **43**, 592–7.

Finley, M. H., and Lee, T. A. (1981). The terminated executive: it's like dying. *Personnel and Guidance Journal*, **59** (6), 382–4.

Fraser, C. (1980). The social psychology of unemployment. In M. A. Jeeves (ed.), *Psychological Survey, No 3*. George Allen and Unwin, London.

French, J. R. P., and Caplan, R. D. (1973). Organizational stress and individual strain. In A. J. Marrow (ed.), *The Failure of Success*. Amacom, New York.

Friedlander, F. (1968). Researcher–subject alienation in behaviour research. In E. Goff and M. W. Shelly (eds), *The Research Society*. Gordon & Breach, New York.

Fromm, E. (1942). *The Fear of Freedom*. Allen & Unwin, London.

Fromm, E. (1947). Personality in the market place. In D. Weir (ed.), (1973), *Men and Work in Modern Britain*. Fontana, London.

Gallagher, J. J. (1980). How executives react to being fired. *Iron Age*, 21 January.

Goffman, E. (1963). *Stigma*. Prentice Hall, New York.

Goldberg, D. P. (1972). *The Detection of Psychiatric Illness by Questionnaire*. Maudsley Monographs, 22, Oxford University Press, London.

Goodchilds, J. D., and Smith, E. F. (1963). The effects of unemployment as mediated by social status. *Sociometry*, **26**, 287–93.

Gouldner, A. (1969). The unemployed self. In R. Fraser (ed.), *Work: Twenty Personal Accounts*. Penguin, Harmondsworth.

Hall, O. M. (1933). Attitudes of unemployed engineers. *Personnel Journal*, **12**, 222–8.

Harré, R. (1978). Accounts, actions and meanings: the practice of participatory psychology. In M. Brenner and P. Marsh (eds), *The Social Contexts of Method*. Croom Helm, New York.

Harrison, R. (1973). Towards a strategy for helping redundant managers. *Management Education and Development*, **4** (2), 77–85.

Harrison, R. (1976). The demoralising experience of prolonged unemployment. *Department of Employment Gazette*, **LXXXIV** (4), 339–48.

Hartley, J. (1979). The personality of unemployed managers: myths and measurement. Unpublished paper, Medical Research Council Social and Applied Psychology Unit, Sheffield University, Memo. no. 257.

Hartley, J. (1980). The impact of unemployment upon the self esteem of managers. *Journal of Occupational Psychology*, **53**, 147–55.

Hartley, J., and Cooper, C.L. (1976). Redundancy: a psychological problem? *Personnel Review*, **5**, 44–8.

Hayes, J., and Nutman, P. (1981). *Understanding the Unemployed*. Tavistock Publications, London.

Helmreich, R. (1972). Stress, self esteem, and attitudes. In B. T. King and E. McGinnies (eds), *Attitudes, Conflict and Social Change*. Academic Press, New York.

Hewitt, J. P. (1979). *Self and Society*. Allyn & Bacon, Boston, Mass.

Hill, J. M. M. (1977). *The Social and Psychological Impact of Unemployment*. Tavistock Institute of Human Relations, London.

Hill, J. M. M. (1978). The psychological impact of unemployment. *New Society*, 19th January, pp. 118–120.

Hopson, B., and Adams, J. (1976). Towards an understanding of transition. In J. Adams, J. Hayes, and B. Hopson (eds), *Transition*. Martin Robertson, London.

Howard, A., and Scott, R. A. (1965). A proposed framework for the analysis of stress in the human organism. *Behavioral Science*, **10**, 141–66.

150

Huczynski, A. (1978). Unemployed managers—a homogeneous group? *Management Education and Development*, **9**, 21–5.

Hyman, M. M. (1979). The effects of unemployment: a neglected problem in modern social research. In R. K. Merton, J. S. Coleman, and P. H. Rossi (eds), *Qualitative and Quantitative Social Research*. Free Press, New York.

Ilfield, F. W. (1976). Characteristics of current social stressors. *Psychological Reports*, **39**, 1231–47.

Israeli, N. (1935). Distress in the outlook of the Lancashire and Scottish unemployed. *Journal of Applied Psychology*, **19** (1), 67–9.

Jaco, E. G. (1970). Mental illness in response to stress. In S. Levine and N. A. Scotch (eds), *Social Stress*. Aldine, Chicago.

Jahoda, M. (1979). The impact of unemployment in the 1930's and in the 1970's. *Bulletin of the British Psychological Society*, **32**, 309–14.

Jahoda, M., and Rush, H. (1980). *Work, Employment and Unemployment*. Science Policy Research Unit Occasional Paper No. 12, University of Sussex.

Jenkins, C., and Sherman, B. (1979). *The Collapse of Work*. Eyre Methuen, London.

Kahn, H. R. (1964). *The Repercussions of Redundancy*. Allen & Unwin, London.

Kasl, S. V., Gore, S., and Cobb, S. (1975). The experience of losing a job: reported changes in health, symptoms and illness behaviour. *Psychosomatic Medicine*, **37**, 106–22.

Kets de Vries, M. F. R. (1978). The midcareer conundrum. *Organizational Dynamics*, **7** (2), 45–62.

Lazarus, R. S. (1966). *Psychological Stress and the Coping Process*. McGraw-Hill, New York.

Leavy, S. A., and Freedman, L. Z. (1961). Psychopathology and occupation. Part 1. Economic insecurity. *Occupational Psychology*, **35**, 23–35.

Levi, L. (ed.) (1971). *Society, Stress and Disease—psychological environment and psychosomatic diseases*. Oxford University Press, London.

Little, C. B. (1973). *Stress Response among Unemployed Technical Professionals*. Ph.D. thesis, Durham, University of New Hampshire.

Little, C.B. (1976). Technical–professional unemployment: middle class adaptability to personal crisis. *Sociological Quarterly*, **17**, 262–74.

Mangham, I. L. (1982). The research enterprise. In N. Nicholson and T. Wall (eds), *The Theory and Practice of Organizational Psychology*, Academic Press, London.

Martin, R., and Fryer, R.H. (1973). *Redundancy and Paternalist Capitalism*. Allen & Unwin, London.

Maurer, H. (1979). *Not Working: an oral history of the unemployed*. Holt, Rinehart, & Winston, New York.

McGivern, C. K., and Fineman, S. (1981). Research and consultancy: towards a conceptual synthesis. Unpublished paper, Centre for the Study of Organizational Change and Development, University of Bath.

Mines, H. Y. (1979). The unemployed senior executive. *Business Horizon*, **22**, (5), 39–40.

Oates, D. (1972). The shattered world of discarded managers. *International Management*, **27** (2), 16–20.

Parker, S. (1975). The effects of redundancy. In B. Esland, G. Salaman, and M. Speakman (eds), *People and Work*. Holmes McDougall, Edinburgh.

Porter, A. (1977). The myth of managerial tenure. *Management Today*, **126**, 63–5.

Powell, D. H., and Driscoll, S. P. F. (1973). Middle class professionals face unemployment. *Society*, **10** (2), 18–26.

Pym, D. (1981). 'Emancipation and organization'. Unpublished paper, London Business School.

Ragland-Sullivan, E., and Barglow, P. (1981). Job loss: psychological response of university faculty. *Journal of Higher Education*, **52** (1), 45–66.

Rosenberg, M. (1965). *Society and the Adolescent Self Image*. Princeton University Press, Princeton, NJ.

Schlozman, K. L., and Verba, S. (1979). *Injury to Insult*. Harvard University Press, Cambridge, Mass.

Seglow, P. (1970). Reactions to redundancy: the influence of the work situation. *Industrial Relations Journal*, **1** (2), 7–22.

Selbourne, D. (1982). Wolverhampton on ice. *New Society*, 21 January.

Selye, H. (1956). *The stress of Life*. McGraw-Hill, New York.

Shanthamani, V. S. (1973). Unemployment and neuroticism. *Indian Journal of Social Work*, **34** (1), 83–102.

Sinfield, A. (1968). *The Long Term Unemployed*. OECD, Paris.

Sinfield, A. (1981a). *What Unemployment Means*. Martin Robertson, Oxford.

Sinfield, A. (1981b). Unemployment in an unequal society. In B. Showler and A. Sinfield (eds), *The Workless State*. Martin Robertson, Oxford.

Speakman, M. A. (1980). Occupational choice and placement. In G. Esland and G. Salaman (eds), *The Politics of Work and Occupations*. Open University Press, Milton Keynes.

Strange, W. G. (1978). Job loss: a psychosocial study of worker reactions to a plant closing in a company town in Southern Appalachia. Testimony before US House of Representatives, Washington, DC.

Ryan,   (1971). *Blaming the Victim*. Pantean Books, Random House New York.

Swinburne, P. (1981). The psychological impact of unemployment on managers and professional staff. *Journal of Occupational Psychology*, **54**, 47–64.

Tausky, C., and Piedmont, E. B. (1967). The meaning of work and unemployment: implications for mental health. *International Journal of Social Psychiatry*, **14**, 44–9.

Thomas, B., and Madigan, C. (1974). Strategy and job choice after redundancy. *Sociological Review*, **22** (1), 83–102.

Torbert, W. (1976). *Creating a Community of Inquiry: conflict collaboration, transformation*. Wiley, New York.

Trades Union Congress (1981). *Centres for the unemployed*. Bulletins Nos 3–6, June–December.

Wedderburn, D. (1964) *White Collar Redundancy*, Cambridge University Press, Cambridge.

White, R. (1959). Motivation reconsidered: the concept of competence. *Psychological Review*, **66**, 287–333.

Wilcock, R. C., and Franke, W. H. (1963). *Unwanted Workers: permanent layoffs and long-term unemployment*. Free Press of Glencoe, New York.

Wood, S. (1977). Is redundancy a social problem? A comment. *Personnel Review*, **6**, 55–9.

Zawadski, B., and Lazarsfeld, P. F. (1935). The psychological consequences of unemployment. *Journal of Social Psychology*, **6**, 224–51.

Index

154